ALCOHOL
Opposing Viewpoints®

OTHER BOOKS OF RELATED INTEREST

OPPOSING VIEWPOINTS SERIES

Biomedical Ethics
Chemical Dependency
Drug Abuse
Health and Fitness
Health Care in America
Mental Illness
Suicide
War on Drugs

CURRENT CONTROVERSIES SERIES

Alcoholism
Drug Trafficking
Gambling
Illegal Drugs
Smoking
Teen Addiction

AT ISSUE SERIES

Legalizing Drugs
Smoking

ALCOHOL
Opposing Viewpoints®

David L. Bender, Publisher
Bruno Leone, Executive Editor
Brenda Stalcup, Managing Editor
Scott Barbour, Senior Editor, Book Editor

OPPOSING VIEWPOINTS® SERIES

'99

Greenhaven Press, Inc., San Diego, California

Cover photo: Craig MacLain

Library of Congress Cataloging-in-Publication Data

Alcohol : opposing viewpoints / Scott Barbour, book editor.
    p.   cm. — (Opposing viewpoints series)
    Includes bibliographical references and index.
    ISBN 1-56510-675-X (lib. bdg. : alk. paper). —
ISBN 1-56510-674-1 (pbk. : alk. paper)
    1. Drinking of alcoholic beverages. 2. Alcohol—Health aspects.
3. Advertising—Alcoholic beverages. 4. Alcoholism—Treatment.
I. Barbour, Scott, 1963– . II. Series.
HV5035.A458 1998
362.292—dc21   97-14487
                                                CIP

Greenhaven Press, Inc., P.O. Box 289009
San Diego, CA 92198-9009

"CONGRESS SHALL MAKE NO LAW...ABRIDGING THE FREEDOM OF SPEECH, OR OF THE PRESS."

First Amendment to the U.S. Constitution

The basic foundation of our democracy is the First Amendment guarantee of freedom of expression. The Opposing Viewpoints Series is dedicated to the concept of this basic freedom and the idea that it is more important to practice it than to enshrine it.

CONTENTS

WHY CONSIDER OPPOSING VIEWPOINTS?

"The only way in which a human being can make some approach to knowing the whole of a subject is by hearing what can be said about it by persons of every variety of opinion and studying all modes in which it can be looked at by every character of mind. No wise man ever acquired his wisdom in any mode but this."

John Stuart Mill

In our media-intensive culture it is not difficult to find differing opinions. Thousands of newspapers and magazines and dozens of radio and television talk shows resound with differing points of view. The difficulty lies in deciding which opinion to agree with and which "experts" seem the most credible. The more inundated we become with differing opinions and claims, the more essential it is to hone critical reading and thinking skills to evaluate these ideas. Opposing Viewpoints books address this problem directly by presenting stimulating debates that can be used to enhance and teach these skills. The varied opinions contained in each book examine many different aspects of a single issue. While examining these conveniently edited opposing views, readers can develop critical thinking skills such as the ability to compare and contrast authors' credibility, facts, argumentation styles, use of persuasive techniques, and other stylistic tools. In short, the Opposing Viewpoints Series is an ideal way to attain the higher-level thinking and reading skills so essential in a culture of diverse and contradictory opinions.

In addition to providing a tool for critical thinking, Opposing Viewpoints books challenge readers to question their own strongly held opinions and assumptions. Most people form their opinions on the basis of upbringing, peer pressure, and personal, cultural, or professional bias. By reading carefully balanced opposing views, readers must directly confront new ideas as well as the opinions of those with whom they disagree. This is not to simplistically argue that everyone who reads opposing views will—or should—change his or her opinion. Instead, the series enhances readers' understanding of their own views by encouraging confrontation with opposing ideas. Careful examination of others' views can lead to the readers' understanding of the logical inconsistencies in their own opinions, perspective on why they hold an opinion, and the consideration of the possibility that their opinion requires further evaluation.

EVALUATING OTHER OPINIONS

To ensure that this type of examination occurs, Opposing Viewpoints books present all types of opinions. Prominent spokespeople on different sides of each issue as well as well-known professionals from many disciplines challenge the reader. An additional goal of the series is to provide a forum for other, less known, or even unpopular viewpoints. The opinion of an ordinary person who has had to make the decision to cut off life support from a terminally ill relative, for example, may be just as valuable and provide just as much insight as a medical ethicist's professional opinion. The editors have two additional purposes in including these less known views. One, the editors encourage readers to respect others' opinions—even when not enhanced by professional credibility. It is only by reading or listening to and objectively evaluating others' ideas that one can determine whether they are worthy of consideration. Two, the inclusion of such viewpoints encourages the important critical thinking skill of objectively evaluating an author's credentials and bias. This evaluation will illuminate an author's reasons for taking a particular stance on an issue and will aid in readers' evaluation of the author's ideas.

As series editors of the Opposing Viewpoints Series, it is our hope that these books will give readers a deeper understanding of the issues debated and an appreciation of the complexity of even seemingly simple issues when good and honest people disagree. This awareness is particularly important in a democratic society such as ours in which people enter into public debate to determine the common good. Those with whom one disagrees should not be regarded as enemies but rather as people whose views deserve careful examination and may shed light on one's own.

Thomas Jefferson once said that "difference of opinion leads to inquiry, and inquiry to truth." Jefferson, a broadly educated man, argued that "if a nation expects to be ignorant and free . . . it expects what never was and never will be." As individuals and as a nation, it is imperative that we consider the opinions of others and examine them with skill and discernment. The Opposing Viewpoints Series is intended to help readers achieve this goal.

David L. Bender & Bruno Leone,
Series Editors

INTRODUCTION

"Beverage alcohol, America's drug of choice, imposes
enormous economic, health and social costs on the nation
each year."

—George A. Hacker and Laura Anne Stuart

"In many situations drink is a joy and a privilege."

—Carey Burkett

In the late 1890s, in the towns of Kansas, a woman named
Carry Nation began to wreck saloons, which were illegal in that
"dry" state. Using rocks and metal bars, she smashed liquor
supplies, furniture, and fixtures. By the early 1900s, Nation had
become famous for swinging a hatchet, which had become her
signature tool, in saloons throughout New York, Washington,
D.C., San Francisco, and other American cities.

Having previously been unhappily married to an alcoholic,
Nation was among the most visible members of the prohibition
movement, who believed that alcohol should be outlawed because it contributed to violence, crime, and the destruction of
families. The movement eventually succeeded; in 1920, the Eigh-
teenth Amendment to the U.S. Constitution took effect, banning
the manufacture and sale of alcoholic beverages. However, Prohibition could not eliminate the public's thirst for beer and spirits.
The law merely drove drinking underground while creating opportunities for bootleggers, dishonest government officials, and
corrupt police officers to profit from the illegal alcohol trade.
Widely regarded as a failure, Prohibition was repealed in 1933.

The story of Carry Nation and the prohibitionist movement illustrates America's ambivalent attitude toward alcohol. The prohi-
bitionists were partially successful because many Americans
shared their view that the excessive use of alcohol brought destructive consequences. On the other hand, the public's demand
for alcoholic beverages proved stronger than the force of law.
These conflicting societal forces are reflected in contemporary
debates about alcohol. Many commentators and public health experts emphasize alcohol's potential to harm individuals, families,
and society. Others insist that, when consumed responsibly and
in moderation, alcohol can be harmless or even beneficial.

On the positive side, alcohol is a key ingredient in many cultural and social customs that bring and hold people together. For
example, drinks are served to break the ice and encourage social

interaction at parties. At weddings, family members and friends express their shared love and hope by offering a champagne toast to the newlyweds. Wine is a central component in many religious rituals that unite congregations in their shared faith. In Europe, wine is commonly served to all family members—including children—when they gather for the evening meal. In the words of Ian Hindmarch, a professor of psychopharmacology at the University of Surrey in England, alcohol "eases and amplifies the joyful occasions of life." The presence of alcoholic beverages at these occasions suggests that alcohol, symbolically as well as literally, helps to hold society together.

In addition to its role in promoting social cohesion, alcohol, when consumed moderately, can have a positive effect on human health. Commentators frequently refer to the "French paradox": Despite having diets high in cholesterol, the French have lower rates of heart disease than do Americans—a disparity that has been attributed to the fact that the French also drink more wine. Numerous studies have substantiated the claim that moderate drinking lowers the risk for coronary heart disease in some individuals. According to R. Curtis Ellison, "Almost every follow-up epidemiologic study has demonstrated that individuals who drink small to moderate amounts of alcohol have a lower risk than nondrinkers of dying from coronary heart disease." Based on these findings, in 1995 the U.S. government for the first time acknowledged the health benefits of alcohol in its nutrition guidelines.

While alcohol offers these and other societal and health benefits, it can also be the source of significant harm. Indeed, many public health experts insist that the risks associated with alcohol far outweigh the benefits. Some commentators focus on the problem of drunk driving: Mothers Against Drunk Driving (MADD) predicts that "about two out of every five Americans will be involved in an alcohol-related crash at some time in their lives." Others focus on alcohol's role in social problems such as violent crime, suicide, domestic violence, and rape. The National Council on Alcoholism and Drug Dependence (NCADD) states that "alcohol is typically found in the offender, victim or both in about half of all homicides and serious assaults, as well as in a high percentage of sex-related crimes, robberies, and incidents of domestic violence." Furthermore, according to the NCADD, "Alcohol-related problems are disproportionately found among both juvenile and adult criminal offenders."

One of the most tragic negative consequences of alcohol abuse is addiction. Although it is believed that not all drinkers are at risk for addiction, a significant number of people do develop drinking problems. The NCADD estimates that 13.8 million adult Americans have problems with drinking and that out of this number, 8.1 million are alcoholics. Alcoholics who do not receive treatment are prone to various severe health conditions, such as liver diseases, cardiovascular diseases, and some forms of cancer. In addition to physical damage, as alcoholics continue to drink, they usually experience an increasing number of problems in their personal lives, including job loss or estrangement from family members. Families are especially strained—and are often destroyed—by the presence of a problem drinker. According to the Entertainment Industries Council, an organization that seeks to educate the public and the entertainment media about alcohol and alcohol-related problems, "Alcoholism contributes to emotional stress and instability for everyone in the family." In these cases, alcohol does not help to hold families together; instead, it tears them apart.

Since alcohol brings both benefits and problems, its widespread use in contemporary society continues to provoke praise as well as criticism. These divergent views are voiced by many of the authors in *Alcohol: Opposing Viewpoints*, which contains the following chapters: Is Alcohol Beneficial for Human Health? Does the Alcohol Industry Market Its Products Responsibly? How Should Alcoholism Be Treated? What Measures Should Be Taken to Reduce Alcohol-Related Problems? Throughout this anthology, authors debate the effects of alcohol on individuals and society and discuss the most effective way to respond to alcohol-related problems.

CHAPTER 1

IS ALCOHOL BENEFICIAL FOR HUMAN HEALTH?

CHAPTER PREFACE

In 1995, the federal government's Dietary Guidelines for Americans declared that the moderate consumption of alcohol helps prevent coronary heart disease in some individuals. The new guidelines reflect the findings of numerous studies reporting that people who drink moderate amounts of alcohol (defined as one or two drinks per day) have fewer heart attacks and live longer than people who abstain from alcohol. Researchers believe that alcohol lowers the drinker's risk of heart attack because it raises levels of high-density lipoprotein (HDL) cholesterol (commonly referred to as "the good cholesterol") and reduces blood clotting.

Many health experts and alcohol industry representatives have welcomed the new guidelines as confirmation of their contention that alcoholic beverages are safe—even beneficial—when consumed responsibly. These commentators argue that the health benefits of alcohol should be actively promoted in order to combat the popular conception that alcohol is a dangerous drug. Among other proposals, they advocate allowing the alcohol industry to include positive health messages on the labels of alcoholic beverages. The industry points out that its labels are already required to display warnings about the health and safety risks posed by alcohol. According to proponents, adding a comment about alcohol's health benefits would give consumers a more balanced view of the health effects of alcoholic beverages.

Others oppose permitting alcohol beverage producers to print the health benefits of alcohol on their labels. George A. Hacker, director for alcohol policies at the Center for Science in the Public Interest, views the industry's health label effort as an attempt to market alcohol "as health food" in order to encourage consumption and increase sales. Hacker and others argue that such labels would send the public the erroneous message that alcohol is harmless and would thereby invite an increase in alcohol abuse. According to Michael Criqui, a professor of family and preventive medicine at the University of California at San Diego, "If you make broad generalizations about the benefits of drinking, you're going to raise the average consumption of society and get more people abusing alcohol."

The government's dietary guidelines leave little doubt that alcohol, when moderately consumed, can have some health benefits for some people. In the following chapter, authors debate whether these benefits outweigh the overall harms of alcohol and whether they justify advising nondrinkers to take up the alcohol habit.

| "The risk of dying of any cause is lower for individuals who consume moderate amounts of alcohol."

MODERATE DRINKING IS BENEFICIAL FOR HUMAN HEALTH

R. Curtis Ellison

In the following viewpoint, R. Curtis Ellison summarizes the research on alcohol's effect on human health. He contends that while heavy drinking increases a person's risk for various diseases, moderate drinking has positive health consequences—including a reduced risk of coronary heart disease. According to Ellison, studies show that moderate drinkers live longer than nondrinkers. Ellison is a professor of preventive medicine and public health at Boston University School of Medicine.

As you read, consider the following questions:

1. Why were many early studies of alcohol's effects criticized, according to Ellison?
2. According to the author, how does alcohol intake affect the risk of stroke?
3. What evidence does Ellison present to support his contention that the consumption of alcohol is the cause of prolonged life among moderate drinkers?

From R. Curtis Ellison, "Does Moderate Alcohol Consumption Prolong Life?" *Priorities*, Summer 1993. Reprinted with permission from *Priorities*, a publication of the American Council on Science and Health, 1995 Broadway, 2nd Floor, New York, NY 10023-5860.

Through the ages, conventional wisdom has been that the moderate intake of alcoholic beverages is consistent with a long and healthy life. Modern medicine became particularly interested in the effects of alcohol consumption on mortality in the 1950s and '60s when coronary heart disease became a major cause of death in the United States and in most other industrialized countries. Primarily from epidemiologic studies designed to identify factors associated with high death rates from coronary heart disease, it became apparent that these rates were lower among drinkers of small to moderate amounts of alcohol than among non-drinkers. However, these studies did not often explore effects of alcohol consumption on overall mortality rates. Specifically, it was not known whether increases in death from other diseases that are associated with alcohol abuse, such as cirrhosis of the liver and certain cancers, offset the apparent beneficial effects of low to moderate alcohol intake on mortality from coronary heart disease. This viewpoint takes a look at the net effects of drinking alcoholic beverages on the risk of the drinker's death.

ALCOHOL AND CORONARY HEART DISEASE

While searching for the risk factors for coronary heart disease in comparisons among countries as well as among individuals, epidemiologists identified a potential benefit from alcohol consumption on mortality from heart disease. In the past three decades, almost every follow-up epidemiologic study has demonstrated that individuals who drink small to moderate amounts of alcohol have a lower risk than non-drinkers of dying from coronary heart disease. Among drinkers, the categories with the lowest coronary heart disease rates vary across studies, ranging from less than one drink per day to three to five drinks per day. In most studies, individuals who state that they normally consume six or more drinks per day, or who admit to having problems with alcohol abuse, have rates of dying from heart disease higher than both non-drinkers and moderate drinkers.

Many of the early studies were criticized for including in the category of non-drinkers both lifetime abstainers and ex-drinkers. Many ex-drinkers may have given up drinking due to alcoholism or other health problems (including cancer and heart disease) and thus would be expected to have a greater risk of early death. Other follow-up studies have demonstrated, however, that even when only lifetime abstainers or healthy abstainers make up the non-drinker category, the risk of coronary heart disease for non-drinkers is still higher than it is for moderate drinkers.

THE EFFECTS OF ALCOHOL ON OTHER DISEASES

Although there is little doubt that the moderate consumption of alcoholic beverages is associated with a lower risk of coronary heart disease, the risk of death from non-cardiac diseases or other causes depends on how much someone drinks.

Moderate Alcohol Intake: There are a number of diseases or conditions that are often attributed to the use of alcohol (*e.g.*, cirrhosis of the liver, certain types of cancer, accidents). In general, cirrhosis and alcohol-related cancers are associated with alcohol abuse and not with the consumption of small to moderate amounts of alcohol.

However, even moderate amounts of alcohol may be related to the risk of death from hemorrhagic stroke. On the other hand, the risk of thrombotic stroke, the much more common type of stroke in the U.S. and Europe, is reduced by moderate amounts of alcohol. Therefore, the net effect of moderate alcohol intake in these parts of the world is a lowering of the risk of stroke.

Questions still remain on the apparent relation between moderate alcohol intake and breast cancer. Certain studies indicate that the risk of breast cancer in women may increase with only moderate levels of alcohol intake. However, other studies indicate no such relationship. It will require further research to clearly define what role, if any, alcohol plays in breast cancer.

Excessive Alcohol Intake: Alcoholics and other abusers of alcohol generally are at increased risk for a number of diseases and causes of death. Driving while intoxicated causes the most accidental alcohol-related deaths. Rates of suicide are also increased for alcohol abusers. Furthermore, excessive drinkers experience increased rates of oral, pharyngeal, esophageal and stomach cancer. This is presumably due to the direct toxic effect of alcohol, and probably other substances in alcoholic beverages, on the tissues lining the upper gastrointestinal tract. Frequently, rates of such cancers are much higher, or even seen almost exclusively, among drinkers who also smoke cigarettes. Indeed, the combination of heavy drinking and smoking is particularly harmful.

THE EFFECTS OF ALCOHOL CONSUMPTION ON TOTAL MORTALITY

One approach to determine the net effects of an exposure (such as alcohol consumption) on disease rates is to calculate the rates for all diseases that may be related to the exposure and then attempt to balance the beneficial and harmful effects. When considering death as the outcome, however, we can simply look at total, or all-cause, mortality to judge the net effects of varying levels of alcohol consumption.

The best way to judge the net effects of alcohol consumption on a variety of causes of death is to look at all-cause mortality in follow-up studies, where data on alcohol use are collected prior to the development of disease or death.

The net effects of alcohol consumption on all-cause mortality were recently reported in nine follow-up cohort studies. All of the studies show that the relative risk of dying from any cause is lower for individuals in at least one category of alcohol consumption than for individuals consuming no alcohol. While the changes were not always statistically significant for each category in each study, the general pattern is very clear. Usually, the lowest risk of death is found in the categories reflecting moderate consumption (one to two drinks per day or individuals classified as "moderate drinkers").

THE RISK OF NOT DRINKING

Many government agencies, public-health organizations and leading medical journals are taking a serious look at the potential health benefits of moderate drinking. More than 100 studies have found that it substantially reduces the risk of coronary heart disease and that moderate drinkers live longer, healthier lives than teetotalers. . . .

An editorial in the *Journal of the American Medical Association* estimates that if Americans stopped drinking altogether, an additional 81,000 people a year would die of heart disease.

John Berlau, *Insight*, March 3, 1997.

Some of the studies included ex-drinkers and lifetime abstainers in the non-drinking category. The greater the proportion of ex-drinkers in the non-drinking category, the higher the death rate is expected to be for that category.

Fortunately, a number of the studies separated the non-drinking category into ex-drinkers and lifetime abstainers. In each of these studies, moderate drinkers had lower death rates than even lifetime abstainers. Results are the same when only healthy abstainers are included in the non-drinking category. Thus, these studies do not support the contention that the inclusion of ex-drinkers or sick individuals in the non-drinking category is the reason that moderate drinkers have lower rates of cardiovascular and other diseases. Overall, the data indicates that, in comparison with non-drinkers (even when the category is limited to healthy, lifetime abstainers), the risk of dying of any cause is lower for individuals who consume moderate amounts of alcohol.

DOES ALCOHOL CONSUMPTION PROLONG LIFE?

In reviewing the results of the studies summarized above, two things become clear. First, individuals who reported that they consumed small to moderate amounts of alcohol had lower death rates than non-drinkers. Thus, on the average, the lives of moderate drinkers were prolonged. The second message from the epidemiologic studies is that those individuals who consumed large amounts of alcohol had higher death rates than non-drinkers (and usually much higher than moderate drinkers). Therefore, on the average, the lives of heavy drinkers were shortened.

How sure can we be that it was the consumption of alcoholic beverages that improved mortality rates in these studies? It is always difficult to prove scientifically that some factor that is associated with an effect causes that effect. It is still possible, though unlikely, that it is not alcohol consumption itself but some lifestyle factor associated with the moderate consumption of alcohol that tends to lead to a prolongation of life.

However, the accumulating evidence strongly suggests that it is the consumption of alcoholic beverages that results in the lower risk of death among moderate drinkers in epidemiologic studies. The evidence includes the following factors:

- a marked consistency of the findings of lower total mortality among drinkers in both men and women, in different ethnic groups and in different geographic areas of the world;
- a consistency across different age groups;
- a reduction of coronary atherosclerosis following alcohol intake in animal studies;
- a large number of identified mechanisms (increase in HDL-cholesterol, decrease in platelet aggregation, etc.) by which alcohol would be expected to reduce the risk of heart disease;
- higher death rates among non-drinkers even when ex-drinkers or individuals with other diseases are excluded.

IMPLICATIONS FOR INDIVIDUALS

Many factors other than alcohol consumption affect life span. Genetics probably plays the largest role in determining longevity. However, diet, smoking habits, physical activity, obesity, use of seat belts and many other lifestyle factors play a role as well. When thinking of alcohol and life span, it is important to remember that any potential prolongation of life associated with moderate drinking varies markedly according to individual characteristics, especially other health-related habits and medical conditions.

Many factors should be taken into account when someone is considering whether or not to drink alcoholic beverages. Inappropriate use can lead to addiction, as well as to an increased risk of accidents, violence and a number of severe and even fatal diseases. The societal and personal costs of alcohol abuse are great. Women at increased risk of breast cancer may decide that it is preferable not to drink because of the possibility of a relation between alcohol and this disease. Thus, it is not possible to make blanket recommendations for everyone in the population.

Even physicians find it difficult to know whether it is safe (or advisable) for a given individual to drink. We must rely on the answers to questions such as, "Is there a family history of alcoholism?" "Has that individual ever abused alcohol or other substances?" "Does heart disease or certain cancers tend to run in the family?" "What is the individual's age, sex, body size?" "Is the individual taking medications or ill with a disease?" Such information helps determine how alcohol affects an individual and, to some extent, the risk that the individual will become an abuser of alcohol. We know that, on the average, the consumption of small to moderate amounts of alcohol results in few adverse effects and large beneficial effects in terms of preventing heart disease. However, we can never be sure, *a priori*, that an individual who begins to drink will not become an alcoholic. The decision to drink alcohol must be an individual choice, based not only on average values from epidemiologic studies, but on individual characteristics and the recognition of all of the potential implications of the decision.

"Drinking alcohol does not guarantee
longevity—and it certainly does not
provide immunity against death!"

DRINKING IS HARMFUL FOR HUMAN HEALTH

Albert B. Lowenfels

In recent years, many scientific studies have concluded that the
moderate consumption of alcohol reduces people's risk of coronary heart disease. In the following viewpoint, Albert B. Lowenfels, a professor of surgery at New York Medical College, concedes that moderate drinking can benefit some people; however,
he insists that the overall health risks of drinking outweigh the
benefits. According to Lowenfels, drinking increases the risk of
cirrhosis of the liver, digestive tract diseases, and various forms
of cancer. In addition, he maintains, drinkers are more likely
than nondrinkers to be involved in accidents. Due to the numerous health problems associated with drinking, Lowenfels concludes, doctors should not advise their patients to drink in order
to lower their risk of heart disease.

As you read, consider the following questions:

1. What experiment would clearly illustrate the effect of alcohol
   on health, according to Lowenfels?
2. How does Lowenfels respond to the argument that the
   "French paradox" proves alcohol's beneficial effect on health?
3. What groups does the author cite to illustrate his assertion
   that avoiding alcohol does not interfere with a long, healthy
   life?

From Albert B. Lowenfels, "Should Physicians Recommend Alcohol to Their Patients?
No," Priorities, vol. 8, no. 1, 1996. Reprinted with permission from Priorities, a publication
of the American Council on Science and Health, 1995 Broadway, 2nd Floor, New York,
NY 10023-5860.

If physicians were to encourage their patients to drink alcohol, what patients would be the target group? Certainly not heavy drinkers, whose health, job and family may already suffer from alcohol abuse or addiction; the advice for these unfortunate individuals should be to reduce alcohol consumption or, preferably, to abstain entirely from alcohol.

Light and moderate drinkers need no encouragement to drink alcohol; instead, they need advice about safe levels for drinking, the dangers of drinking while driving or operating motorized equipment and, for females, the necessity for abstinence from alcohol prior to conception and during pregnancy.

The only target group, therefore, would be those patients who are nonconsumers of alcohol. Physicians would never advocate alcohol consumption for children, so our advice would be limited to nondrinking adults. The size of this group can be estimated as follows: There are currently about 200 million adults in the United States. Although the exact number of nondrinkers in that population is unknown, a good estimate is about 25 to 30 percent, or at least 50 million persons.

We know that this large group of nondrinkers includes many different subgroups. Some nonconsumers avoid alcohol because they already suffer from an alcohol-related disease. Others abstain because they have a chronic disease and have been advised to avoid alcohol. A third group may have an alcoholic parent and intuitively know they must avoid alcohol. A final group abstains from alcohol because of religious convictions. Clearly, it would be unwise to recommend light or moderate drinking to patients in any of these categories.

ALCOHOL AND HEALTH

What about the residual group of nondrinkers who have no definite reason to avoid alcohol? Would their health improve if they began drinking? To give a thoughtful answer to this important question, we must first review the complex relationship between alcohol and health. What are the detrimental effects of alcohol consumption and what, if any, are its health benefits? This problem has attracted an enormous amount of interest: In the past few years thousands of articles have been published on alcohol and health.

Alcohol consumers are known to have increased risks for many diseases. These include cirrhosis of the liver; digestive-tract diseases such as ulcers or pancreatitis; several painful and often lethal cancers such as throat cancer, esophageal cancer and liver cancer; and certain neurologic disorders such as blackouts and seizures. In addition, all types of accidents, including fatal car crashes, are more frequent in drinkers than in nondrinkers. Finally, fetal alcohol syndrome, now thought to be the most common cause of mental retardation, occurs only in the children of alcohol consumers. While it is true that some of these health problems occur primarily in heavy drinkers, any amount of alcohol may be hazardous for other diseases such as fetal alcohol syndrome, for which a safe, lower limit is unknown.

There is only one well-recognized health "benefit" of alcohol consumption: Health professionals now agree that drinking small amounts of alcohol seems to reduce the risk of coronary heart disease. But is this single gain enough to balance the long list of alcohol-associated health problems?

WEAK EVIDENCE

We could find a convincing answer to the overall impact of alcohol on health if we were able to conduct the following experiment, a prospective randomized trial. Nondrinking adults would be randomly assigned to one of two groups: an alcohol-consuming group in which all the participants would be required to drink a daily glass of fruit juice spiked with about an ounce or two of alcohol, and a second, "control" group who would drink only fruit juice without alcohol. The two groups would be followed for 10 or 20 years so that we could compare the death rates in alcohol consumers to the rates in nonconsumers.

For various ethical and practical reasons, this experiment—which would give us badly needed information about the potential health benefits of light or moderate drinking—will never be performed. Therefore, to answer the "to drink or not to drink" question, we're forced to rely upon indirect, weaker evidence from nonrandomized trials—retrospective studies that look back at past alcohol exposure and cross-cultural studies that compare drinking levels and health status among different groups. These types of studies can be plagued by confounding and bias.

If we accept the premise that alcohol protects against certain types of heart disease, will we gain or lose by telling our nondrinking patients they should drink? We know that there are already at least 100,000 alcohol-related deaths each year in the United States. It is difficult to predict the number of heart disease deaths caused by alcohol abstinence, but the number has been estimated to be approximately equal to the number of alcohol-related deaths. Thus, a health policy of advocating light or moderate drinking for our abstinent patients would be unlikely to save many lives.

According to a report prepared for the Robert Wood Johnson Foundation, the cost of alcohol addiction for the year 1990 in the United States amounted to almost 100 billion dollars—higher than the estimated 67 billion dollars we spend for illicit drugs and the 72 billion dollars we spend for tobacco addiction. An unpredictable number of new alcohol consumers would eventually turn into heavy drinkers or become addicted to alcohol, requiring additional funds to cover the costs of their alcohol-related problems.

THE FRENCH PARADOX?

Advocates for moderate drinking often speak of the "French paradox." In the southwest of France—despite high consumption of foods rich in cholesterol, such as buttery sauces, various cheeses and goose liver—the risk of heart disease, particularly in men, appears to be lower than expected. According to moderate-drinking advocates, this "paradox" of a high-cholesterol diet and a low risk of heart disease can be explained by the beneficial, protective effect of copious amounts of alcohol—particularly red wine.

But men in France actually die about two years earlier than do men in Sweden or Norway, even though per capita alcohol consumption in Scandinavia is only about one third the consumption in France. Frenchmen, although they may not be dying of heart disease, are dying of other causes. Drinking alcohol does not guarantee longevity—and it certainly does not provide immunity against death!

BENEFIT OR RISK?

It could be that the alcohol itself is of no health benefit. One study claims that the benefits of drinking are limited to red wine. Red wine has a variety of nonalcoholic compounds that could include the coronary disease preventive.

Weigh this against the risks associated with drinking, even moderate drinking: stroke, breast cancer, birth defects, hypertension, alcoholism, car accidents.

Suzanne Jennings, Forbes, September 13, 1993.

And what has been the health experience of groups of individuals who have been lifelong abstainers? Do they die prematurely? Do they suffer from excess heart disease or other illnesses? Fortunately, such information is available from many reports reviewing the health of Seventh Day Adventists and Mormons—groups that abstain from alcohol on religious grounds. Their survival rates are generally higher than the American average. Avoiding alcohol does not interfere with an active, prolonged, healthy life.

From available statistics we know that there are more female than male nondrinkers. We also know that women are more likely to develop complications of alcohol, such as liver cirrhosis, at lower levels of alcohol intake than men. We therefore can predict that a policy of telling our nondrinking patients to begin drinking would be likely to yield more alcohol-related complications in women than in men.

There are many readily available nonaddictive drugs that effectively reduce the risk of coronary-artery occlusion. Why, then, should we recommend a drug that we know leads to loss of control or alcohol addiction in about 10 percent of users? It makes little sense to recommend alcohol as a safeguard against coronary heart disease when there are so many much safer drugs already at hand.

As we focus on the problem of alcohol and public health, we can learn a great deal by reviewing recommendations from organizations with recognized expertise in this area.

In 1991 the World Health Organization assembled a special review group to formulate worldwide alcohol policy. The group's conclusion on drinking and heart disease was this: "Any attempt to put across a message which encourages drinking on the basis of hoped-for gains in coronary heart disease prevention would be likely to result in more harm than benefit to the population."

In the United States, the National Institute on Alcohol Abuse and Alcoholism warns us that vulnerability to alcoholism and alcohol-related pathologies varies among individuals and cannot always be predicted before a patient begins to drink.

Finally, the Christopher D. Smithers Foundation, the largest private philanthropic organization devoted to research on alcoholism in America, does not advocate light or moderate drinking as a public health measure.

Over 2,000 years ago Hippocrates, one of our wisest physicians, reminded us, "Above all, do no harm." Let us remember this prudent advice as we decide what we should tell our patients about alcohol and health.

> "While the federal government says moderate alcohol intake can prolong life, public schools and the government-funded 'anti-abuse' apparatus treat alcohol like rat poison."

THE HEALTH BENEFITS OF ALCOHOL SHOULD BE PROMOTED MORE VIGOROUSLY

Dave Shiflett

The U.S. federal dietary guidelines state that moderate drinking lowers the risk for coronary heart disease in some individuals. However, Dave Shiflett argues in the following viewpoint, despite these guidelines, the education system and the government's regulatory agencies continue to characterize alcohol as a drug that is always dangerous. Shiflett, a writer who lives in northern Virginia, concludes that the health benefits of alcohol should be publicly acknowledged by educators and policy makers.

As you read, consider the following questions:

1. What recommendations does the report "Sensible Drinking" make for men, according to Shiflett?
2. According to Shiflett, what are students taught about drinking alcohol?
3. In the author's opinion, why could allowing health benefits labels on alcoholic beverages "balance the picture"?

Said Aristotle unto Plato,
"Have another sweet potato?"
Said Plato unto Aristotle,
"Thank you, I prefer the bottle."
—Owen Wister

W ere America's students still burdened with the duty of rote memorization, we can nevertheless be assured they wouldn't be asked to learn a ditty so dangerous as Mr. Wister's. Quite the contrary. Anyone who spouted such sentiments in a contemporary classroom might find that the rules against washing out young mouths with soap can be lifted on special occasions.

Consider the case of poor Shannon Eierman, a 16-year-old honor student and all-county softball player at Atholton (Md.) High School. On a school ski trip to Vermont in February 1996, Eierman walked into the room of some friends and discovered they were drinking beer. Hoping to avoid trouble, she grabbed two beers and began pouring them out.

Too late. Chaperones suddenly appeared; soon a dozen or so of the youngsters had been relieved of their ski passes and forced to write detailed accounts of their transgressions. Seven of the guilty, including Eierman, were suspended from school, she for five days. Shannon was also forced to attend an alcohol treatment program and was banned from extracurricular activities for two quarters—a punishment that may have cost her a sports scholarship.

It could have been worse. Shannon had actually received the minimum punishment under Howard County's "zero tolerance" program. As the *Washington Post* reported, "Last year, Howard officials provoked an uproar when they suspended students who drank a glass of wine with dinner in France on a school trip."

A HARSH STANCE

For a generation steeped in mescaline, marijuana, and tequila shooters, the baby boomers take a fanatically harsh stance on beer drinking by their children—harsher, indeed, than the stiff old Puritans who proclaimed drink a "gift from God." Students who bring even a non-alcoholic beer to a Fairfax County (Va.) school face suspension, even though those concoctions' alcohol content is only .5 percent. (By way of comparison, one study indicates that after three days in the refrigerator, Dole pineapple juice becomes .34 percent alcohol.)

And nationwide, alcohol education campaigns have not shied

from comparing booze use to cocaine snorting. Indeed, one poster, featuring a bottle of beer tipped by a hypodermic needle, carries this message: "Beer contains alcohol. Alcohol is a drug. Alcohol is the number one drug problem in the country. Not marijuana. Not cocaine. Alcohol. Talk to your kids about alcohol."

In fidelity to Uncle Sam's auntish predilections, the latest edition of the official United States nutritional guidelines warns that drinking can lead to high blood pressure, cancer, "accidents, violence, suicides, birth defects, and overall mortality." Yet the guidelines also declare, in a stunning turnaround, that "moderate drinking is associated with lower risk for Coronary Heart Disease in some individuals." This is a significant change from earlier statements that alcohol had "no benefit" and suggestions to avoid any level of drinking whatsoever. It also gives rise to an amusing paradox: While the federal government says moderate alcohol intake can prolong life, public schools and the government-funded "anti-abuse" apparatus treat alcohol like rat poison. All of which raises at least two interesting questions: What does the scientific evidence tell us, and what effect does this evidence have on public policy?

MODERATE DRINKING IS GOOD FOR MOST PEOPLE

There is nothing new about health claims for alcohol. Among the most extravagant were made on behalf of distilled spirits by one Hieronymous Brunschwig, who practiced medicine in fifteenth-century Germany:

> It eases diseases coming of cold. It comforts the heart. It heals all old and new sores on the head. It causes a good color in a person. It heals baldness and causes the hair well to grow, and kills lice and fleas. It cures lethargy. . . . It eases the pain in the teeth, and causes sweet breath. It heals the canker in the mouth, in the teeth, in the lips, and in the tongue. It causes the heavy tongue to become light and well-speaking. It heals the short breath. It causes good digestion and appetite for to eat, and takes away all belching. It draws the wind out of the body . . .

Nowadays the claims are not quite so grandiose, yet the idea is the same: Moderate drinking is good for most people. A March 1996 article in the British Medical Journal offered this overview: "The inverse association between moderate alcohol consumption and coronary heart disease is well established. Evidence for a causal interpretation comes from over 60 ecological, case-control, and cohort studies."

Indeed, anyone requesting similar evidence will have it delivered by the truckload. The Harvard Medical School analyzed 200 studies and found that moderate drinking is associated with as much as a 45 percent reduced risk of heart disease. The Honolulu Heart Study put the decrease at 50 percent. When "60 Minutes" did a story on the subject, it broadcast this hearty endorsement by Dr. Curtis Ellison of the Boston School of Medicine: "I think the data are now so convincing that the total mortality rates are lower among moderate drinkers. It seems quite clear that we should not do anything that would decrease moderate drinkers in the population."

ABANDON TEETOTALING

So convinced is the British government of the benefits of moderate drinking that it actually suggests that older abstainers abandon their teetotaling. The UK guidelines, called "Sensible Drinking," make these recommendations for men:

- The health benefit from drinking relates to men aged over 40 and the major part of this can be obtained at levels as low as one unit a day with the maximum health advantage lying between one and two units a day.

- Regular consumption of between three and four units a day by men of all ages will not accrue significant health risks.

- Consistently drinking four or more units a day is not advised as a sensible drinking level because of the progressive health risk it carries.

Because women tend to be lighter than men, and because their bodies contain a lower proportion of water which results in higher tissue concentration of alcohol, their guidelines are somewhat more stringent:

- The health benefit from drinking for women relates to post-menopausal women and the major part of this can be obtained at levels as low as one unit a day, with the maximum health advantage lying between one and two units a day.

- Regular consumption of between two and three units a day by women of all ages will not accrue any significant health risk.

- Consistently drinking three or more units a day is not advised as a sensible drinking level because of the progressive health risk it carries.

The good news doesn't stop there. In what will probably be a shock to Americans of both sexes, the UK guidelines even dismiss the idea that pregnant women should abstain: "In the light of the evidence received, our conclusion is that, to minimize risk to the developing fetus, women who are trying to become pregnant or are at any stage of pregnancy, should not drink more than 1 or 2 units of alcohol once or twice a week, and should avoid episodes of intoxication."

From reduction in cholesterol gallstones to lower rates of Ischaemic stroke, "Sensible Drinking" finds many benefits to moderate tippling, including this stunner: "Drinking in the range of 7 units to 40 units a week lowers the risk of [Coronary Heart Disease] by between 30% and 50%." (A British drink is somewhat smaller than an American drink: about 9–10 grams of alcohol vs. 12–14 grams.)

NET SAVINGS

American advocates of healthy drinking have been singing the same song for many years, though not under government auspices. Lewis Perdue, author of *The French Paradox and Beyond* and publisher of *Healthy Drinking* magazine, notes a 1991 Harvard study which found that male doctors who drank on average one-half to one drink per day had 21 percent less coronary artery disease than abstainers, or a relative risk of .79 for the drinkers compared to 1.00 for abstainers. "The relative risk," Perdue crows, "continued to drop with increased consumption. Men who consumed one to one and a half drinks per day reduced their Coronary Artery Disease risk by 32 percent, three to four and a half per day reduced it by 43 percent, and those drinking more than four and a half drinks per day reduced their risk by 59 percent."

Perdue admits that there are trade-offs, even for those who favor moderate drinking. "The World Health Association's statistics for 1989 showed that the U.S. death rate from cirrhosis was 17 per 100,000 while cardiovascular disease killed 464 per 100,000. By contrast, the same study shows France with almost double the cirrhosis rate—31 per 100,000—but with cardiovascular rates at only 310 per 100,000. Using these figures, it is not hard to see that if the U.S. rates were normalized with those of France, 14 more people per 100,000 would die of cirrhosis, but 154 fewer people would die of cardiovascular disease, a net savings of 140 people per 100,000 population who would live longer in order to die of something else.". . .

The new nutritional guidelines were not well received in the dry community. The Center for Science in the Public Interest, which is not interested in the science of moderation, greeted the guidelines with a wagging finger: "Providing information about the scientific evidence, and drawing conclusions about its utility for the general population, are two different issues. . . .

One thing [governments] should not do is provide generalized recommendations. They should give as much attention to what the findings don't say, which is, 'Who won't benefit? And who will be harmed?'"

EDUCATIONAL MESSAGES

The same spirit holds forth among those who design and implement alcohol "awareness" programs in the public schools. When asked if the guidelines will affect school alcohol education policies, Bill Modzeleski, director of the Department of Education's Safe and Drug Free Schools program, which supports programs in 97 percent of the nation's school districts, said, "Probably not. For our population, alcohol is an illegal substance." He thoroughly disagrees with the idea that children are receiving mixed messages from the government on drinking, with schools saying alcohol is bad and the guidelines saying it can prolong life. "Our population doesn't drink for its health effects," he says.

Nor do the youngsters listen to health warnings. "Many students are heavily into binge drinking," Modzeleski says. Drinking remains "pretty steady" and has been "high right along." Maryland officials say that 70.1 percent of seniors in Shannon Eierman's school district reported having a drink within the past twelve months, and nationwide surveys reflect similar consumption patterns.

Schools will, of course, accommodate some of their charges' "inappropriate" behaviors, even to the point of showing them how to don condoms (probably not a revelation to many). Perhaps young tipplers should argue that they're going to drink anyway, so the schools should provide cab fare. In any event, the practice has been to reject any curriculum suggesting there is such a thing as responsible drinking. Instead, students are taught that drinking alcohol in any amount is yet another form of drug use, which has caused more than one family unnecessary friction at the cocktail hour.

LABELS

Children are not the only Americans shielded from the moderate drinking message. While the latest health guidelines carry a reasoned message, few Americans are familiar with them. In the one place such a message would be seen by the greatest number of interested parties—the labels on alcoholic beverages—the good news about moderation suffers blackout.

The Bureau of Alcohol, Tobacco and Firearms, which oversees

the labeling process, is considering attempts to add health messages to the bottles which, by law, must continue to carry the Surgeon General's warnings about alcohol-related health and safety problems. The mildest proposal comes from the Wine Institute, which has petitioned to force labels to suggest that drinkers write off for the nutritional guidelines. The Competitive Enterprise Institute (CEI) is campaigning for a label that reads, "There is significant evidence that moderate consumption of alcoholic beverages may reduce the risk of heart disease." These will not strike many consumers as excessive claims, but ATF is in no hurry to allow changes on bottle labels. Paternalism comes first.

Death Rates for 1989, per 100,000 People

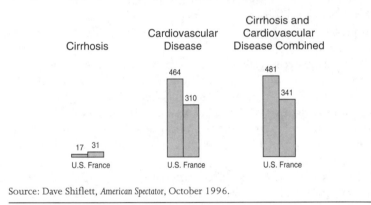

Source: Dave Shiflett, *American Spectator*, October 1996.

"The Wine Institute and others want to put forth a positive attitude about their product," says the highly personable Bill Earle, deputy associate director for regulatory programs at ATF. "They want to move up to the next level. But we're going to be very cautious. A short message could be misleading if it only communicates partial information. Remember, the dietary guidelines refer to good and bad effects of drink."

Because the bottles already contain a health warning, a suggestion of benefits could balance the picture. Yet Earle responds, "Our position with the industry is that the best place to conduct dialogue is in the free press, not necessarily in labeling or advertising by wine companies." In the meantime, he notes, "Dietary guidelines disconnected the language of 'alcohol and other drugs,' which HHS [U.S. Department of Health and Human Services] and others have used for years. That's a subtle but telling observation about the changing view."

Such subtlety is not good enough for CEI's Ben Lieberman, who says his organization is prepared to sue the bureau for not responding in a timely manner to its petition. While fully understandable, CEI should not think that it is being singled out for the glacier treatment. Coors Brewing Company was forced to wage a court battle over the course of eight years to be allowed to include the strength of beers on its labels. The case ended when the Supreme Court ruled 9–0 to allow brewers to disclose the information, thus overcoming a 1935 law that was enacted after Prohibition's repeal.

That victory was not without its ironies, including the fact that not all beer manufacturers initially supported the change. "We think it is suicidal to market a product based on its alcohol content," said August A. Busch IV, vice-president of Anheuser-Busch. Strangely enough, all alcoholic beverages except beer are required to disclose their alcoholic content on their labels.

THE NUMBERS GAME

Ultimately the push to cut alcohol consumption is built on the belief that some 10 percent of American adults have what are called "drinking problems"—a figure that, like every statistic associated with alcohol, is questioned by specialists.

Researcher Joseph E. Josephson, writing in a publication for the Columbia University School of Public Health, has questioned the very idea that there is a large number of problem drinkers in America:

> An objective assessment of government statistics on alcohol-related problems, many of them compiled in the Third Report to the U.S. Congress on Alcohol and Health in 1978, indicates that there is little sound basis for claims that there are upwards of 10 million problem drinkers (including alcoholics) in the adult population and that their number is increasing; that there are 1.5 to 2.25 million problem drinkers among women; that there are over 3 million problem drinkers among youth; that the heavy consumption of alcohol by pregnant women leads consistently to a cluster of birth defects . . . [and] that half of all motor vehicle accident fatalities are alcohol-related. . . . These and other claims about the extent and consequences of alcohol use and abuse—some of them fanciful, others as yet to be supported to research—are part of the "numbers game" which besets discussion of alcohol-related problems and policy.

Epidemiologist Harold A. Mulford, writing in the *Encyclopedic Handbook of Alcoholism*, made a similar charge:

> NIAAA's [National Institute on Alcohol Abuse and Alcoholism]

legislatively mandated reports to Congress contain the official prevalence and distribution data for the nation. They are the most publicized prevalence and distribution conclusions and the ones most often cited by politicians and program policy makers. Their official character, however, is not to be confused with scientific validity. Whether by design or not, the reports to Congress likely reflect a contemporary fact of life. The welfare, perhaps even the survival, of NIAAA, depends on (1) the apparent magnitude of the alcohol problem, and (2) whether it is made to appear that a disease (rather than a moral or social problem) is being attacked.

. . . In recent years the government has undertaken a number of questionable public-safety campaigns, from banning lawn darts (which killed three people over the course of seventeen years) to targeting college coeds with AIDS prevention messages. And while some people should avoid drinking, alcohol's health benefits are no longer a matter of scientific debate. These benefits, presented reasonably, could do much more to enhance the lives of most Americans than all the cod liver oil–type admonitions foisted upon us by our surgeon generals. Plato would no doubt agree.

"Promoting drinking risks increasing overall consumption and the levels of alcohol-related problems throughout society."

THE HEALTH BENEFITS OF ALCOHOL SHOULD NOT BE PROMOTED

George A. Hacker

George A. Hacker is the director for alcohol policies at the Center for Science in the Public Interest, a Washington, D.C., consumer advocacy organization that focuses on food and nutrition policies. He is also a coauthor of the books *The Booze Merchants* and *Marketing Booze to Blacks*. In the following viewpoint, Hacker criticizes dietary guidelines that recommend the moderate consumption of alcohol in order to reduce the risk of heart disease. According to Hacker, such recommendations have allowed the alcohol industry to promote its products as "health food." Although Hacker concedes that the moderate use of alcohol can benefit the health of some drinkers, he insists that promotion of the health benefits of alcohol will result in an increase in alcohol consumption and alcohol-related problems.

As you read, consider the following questions:

1. How should the decision to drink be made, in Hacker's opinion?
2. According to the author, how will alcoholics respond to the news that moderate drinking is beneficial?
3. What lifestyle changes does the author contend should be promoted instead of moderate drinking?

From George A. Hacker, "Making Sense of Health Claims for Alcohol: To Whose Health?" in *Wine in Context: Nutrition, Physiology, Policy—Proceedings of the Symposium on Wine and Health* (Reno, Nevada, June 24–25, 1996), published by the American Society for Enology and Viticulture. Reprinted by permission. (Endnotes in the original have been omitted here.)

Early in 1996, the United States Departments of Health and Human Services and Agriculture issued an update of *Dietary Guidelines for Americans*, which includes a recommendation related to alcohol consumption. The government's advice on drinking says, "If you drink alcoholic beverages, do so in moderation, with meals, and when consumption does not put you or others at risk." That statement, which incorporates certain definitions of moderation, recognizes that most persons who drink modestly run only minor risks related to their drinking, and that for some of them, the regular ingestion of small amounts of alcohol may even provide some health benefit.

Frankly, it's hard to argue against the common sense wisdom in this advice: that there's good in doing all things in moderation. This sensible advice, however, falls short of providing an endorsement of drinking, and far short of a message that those who do not drink should take it up. Yet, that is precisely what the current debate on moderate drinking is all about: increasing consumption of alcoholic beverages, particularly wine; and fattening the coffers of alcoholic-beverage producers. Forgive my cynicism, but I view the campaign to promote the healthfulness of wine through oat-bran and vitamin-supplement lenses.

MARKETING WINE AS HEALTH FOOD

Media boasts of Wine Institute leader John DeLuca confirm a master plan to market wine as a health food. Following the release of the *Dietary Guidelines*, he declared, "'We had a campaign of tenacity, working with the contributions of the scientific community. . . . We have taken [drinking] away from the shadows of the past,' where the industry was seen as a 'sin industry' and into something that is part of a healthy diet" [quoted by Carl Nolte, *San Francisco Chronicle*]. Wine is back on the table and consumption of table wine is expected to rise.

Lobbying federal officials has been only part of an all-out effort to promote increased wine consumption. In the past few years, we have witnessed a broad (if not a centrally orchestrated) campaign to trumpet the healthfulness of drink. The media, in screaming headlines that spread cheer about drinking, has hyped the results of epidemiological studies, frequently promoting the general notion that all but a few consumers should drink for their health. Information about the downsides of alcohol, about addiction and about the numerous individual factors that should inform a decision to drink have been down-played or ignored. One study by researchers at the National Cancer Institute examined popular press coverage of the relationship between alcohol and breast cancer and found that "the vast majority of scientific studies were ignored." The media has not done a very good job in covering this issue, partly because they've been looking at it through rose-colored glasses. For example, the fact that health researchers almost universally hesitate to provide generic recommendations that consumers begin drinking or increase their consumption of alcohol is most often relegated to a final paragraph or utterly forgotten.

AN INGENIOUS CAMPAIGN

The campaign to tout the beneficial effects of moderate alcohol consumption—essentially limited to wine—has been multi-faceted, ingenious, and at times, necessarily subtle. For example, neckhangers for Almaden Wine generously promote contributions to an affiliate of the American Heart Association. These label attachments feature several mentions of the name and well-known symbol of the Association and boast the likeness of centenarian George Burns toasting with a glass of wine. The campaign, notably, proclaims, "A Taste for Life."

GRAPE JUICE VS. BURGUNDY

It's not entirely clear that it's the alcohol in wine that helps the heart. Purple grape juice, for instance, contains more resveratrol—a compound in wine thought to lower cholesterol levels in blood—than many wines. And according to a University of California at Davis study, these non-alcoholic compounds (known as phenolics) may have an important anti-oxidant effect in the body that prevents narrowing of the arteries and the formation of blood clots. So non-alcoholic wine, grapes, grape juice, and raisins may be every bit as good for your ticker as a glass of Burgundy.

Ben Sherwood, *Washington Monthly*, May 1993.

This kind of implied health claim would never pass muster under the Nutrition Labeling and Education Act, which governs food labeling. That law, and other Food and Drug Administration policy, provides guidance for the Bureau of Alcohol, Tobacco, and Firearms' (BATF) assessment of health claims for alcoholic beverages, yet BATF has failed to act against this questionable promotion. It is simply astonishing that we would have stronger standards governing health claims for broccoli than for alcohol, America's leading and most devastating drug.

In 1994, the campaign for healthier profits misappropriated the imprimatur of the World Health Organization (WHO) as an endorser of daily drinking in the Oldways Preservation & Exchange Trust Mediterranean Diet Pyramid, leading to dozens of media stories that incorrectly associated the WHO with a policy it has always opposed. The WHO response to the Diet Pyramid publicity summarily dismissed the concept of risk-free drinking and concluded that the best health message related to alcohol would be "the less you drink, the better."

More recently, in the 1995 *60 Minutes* follow-up of its 1991 "French Paradox" report, the campaign even resorted to scare tactics to get people to drink, when Curtis Ellison warned viewers (originally, attendees at the 1995 WineExpo) that "abstinence is a major risk factor for coronary heart disease."

JUST A WAY TO BOOST SALES

Indeed, campaign spin doctors have been busy, portraying industry's economic incentives as concern for the public health. Economic studies have been commissioned documenting the savings in health care costs; wine interests succeeded in attaching a legislative rider to the bill funding the National Institutes for Health, requiring the National Institute on Alcohol Abuse and Alcoholism to study the health effects of moderate drinking. Another study, reported in the industry trade journal, *Wines and Vines*, provides a rough cost-benefit analysis of mounting a publicity campaign about the health benefits of drinking. Just another way to boost consumption and sales.

Spurred by the controversy, and no doubt anxious to attract clients and supporters, the libertarian Competitive Enterprise Institute, under the twin banners of commercial free speech and free enterprise, has championed the cause of health claims in advertising and labeling, filing a petition with the Bureau of Alcohol, Tobacco, and Firearms. Although the Institute claims that it is not directly representing alcohol interests, its proxy is apparent. The petition has languished at the Department of Treasury; surprisingly, it was not rejected outright.

Admittedly, impressive evidence now demonstrates an epidemiological association between moderate alcohol consumption (and some studies point to wine consumption, in particular) and a reduced risk of coronary heart disease. We have no quarrel with the latest research. The issue before us today, however, is what we make of the evidence. Should it be translated into messages that encourage drinking?

THE PROMOTION OF HEALTH CLAIMS IS NOT JUSTIFIED

In my view, even the current, convincing evidence of health benefits for *some* fails to justify the proposals for health claims in labeling and advertising, and for incorporation into ideal, "Mediterranean" diets or promotional "food pyramids." Simply stated, an unadorned, unqualified statement recommending moderate wine consumption at mealtime (even where "moderate" is defined in *Dietary Guidelines* terms) would tend to mislead and ultimately may cause as much—or more—harm as good. In essence, such proposals represent marketing messages masquerading as health advice.

The attempt to promote wine as just another food group should fail for four reasons:

(1) The benefits of daily, moderate drinking are not universal. Many users would be misled by a simple recommendation to include wine with meals.

(2) Even moderate consumption could place some users at risk.

(3) Alcohol is an addictive drug; moderate drinking could lead to heavier, problematic consumption.

(4) Promoting drinking risks increasing overall consumption and the levels of alcohol-related problems throughout society.

Although some people may benefit, indiscriminate advice to nondrinkers to begin consuming for health reasons would be inappropriate. Healthy, young people not at risk for heart disease would derive no benefit and likely increase their risk of a wide range of alcohol problems that appear to be dose responsive. Is it likely that those consumers, who have been conditioned to drink at all occasions and in most situations by thousands of beer, wine, and liquor ads over the years, as well as their own experience, will stop at two for men or one for women or limit their drinking only to meals?

In short, to recommend wine—or other alcoholic beverage—as part of a healthy diet, without adequate qualification and explanation, would deceive many who stand to gain little or nothing and imperil others whose heavier drinking it would trigger or justify. Though a few non-drinkers might benefit, such information would hardly cause heavier drinkers to tame their consumption. For many, the decision whether to drink should involve consultation with a physician familiar with the patient's family history, health status, medication regimen, and life-style. We should not permit commercially inspired health claims to substitute for balanced public health information about alcohol or take the place of disciplined, individually-focused medical advice.

SUBSTANTIAL RISKS

In considering the utility of such information, we should not forget that, for many, even moderate consumption of alcohol, whether in the form of wine, beer, or liquor, may pose substantial risks. The latest US *Dietary Guidelines* on alcohol uses more than half its allotted space to detail the kinds of people who should not drink at all. These include children and adolescents; people who can't control their drinking; women trying to conceive or who are pregnant; drivers and persons who plan to perform tasks that require attention or skill; and individuals using prescription and over-the-counter medications.

Curiously, older people, who might stand to benefit the most from a modest, daily dose of alcohol, would not be well-served by the ideal diet's suggestion of a drink or two with dinner. Their bodies, higher in fat and lower in concentrations of water, may not tolerate that much alcohol, putting them at risk for crippling falls and innumerable fender-benders, if not worse, at relatively low blood alcohol concentration levels. What kind of message does the half-truth recommendation send the elderly? Older people take the highest levels of medications, including many antidepressants and antihistamines that would react dangerously with alcohol. By the year 2030, people over 60 will comprise 25% of the US population. How will their healthy, *moderate* alcohol consumption affect them and the rest of us?

ALCOHOL AND WOMEN

And what about women, who metabolize and tolerate alcohol differently from men? Even at relatively low levels of steady alcohol consumption, they may increase their risk of breast cancer, alcoholism, and giving birth to a child with potentially serious fetal alcohol effects. The head of Harvard's nutrition department, Walter Willett is "convinced that there's an increased risk of breast cancer at as little as one drink a day." Should young women, whose hearts have little or nothing to gain from drinking, take the risk of drinking daily? Should they, as a 1996 study out of the National Cancer Institute suggests, take the chance that their drinking during pregnancy will increase the risk that their children will develop infant leukemia?

The 1995 Harvard Nurses' Health Study demonstrates that whatever heart benefit for some, moderate drinking has no particular protective effect for women at low risk of heart disease. Promoting a message that lures consumers into believing that a glass or two of Merlot—or maybe three with a long dinner—is a good thing for all actually deceives. The information provides a vague, half truth at best.

Most of the experts recognize that regular, moderate drinking would require some trade-offs for drinkers. On the one hand, moderate drinking might reduce one's risk of coronary heart disease, a substantial risk factor for older men and women. On the other, that same amount of consumption might marginally increase one's risk of other diseases, including certain cancers. Working out the risk-benefit equation is no easy task, particularly when one begins to factor in genetic and environmental influences. A generic recommendation to drink fails to consider these complexities and usurps the role of physicians who are far better qualified to help guide individuals in making such decisions.

ALCOHOL CONSUMPTION WOULD INCREASE

Worst of all in the proposal for alcohol health claims and diet recommendations is the assumption that more drinking would result in a healthier society. Regular, moderate drinking in this country would result in a substantial increase in alcohol consumption. Today, Americans drink very little, and, compared to most industrialized countries, relatively few even drink. To alcohol producers, the 40% of adults who now abstain represent a massive growth market. Of those who drink, fewer than 20% drink on a regular basis. Wine growers and merchants wish that Americans would learn to drink wine like the French, Italians, and other Europeans. The consequences of this increased drinking would be felt throughout society, in higher levels of alcohol-related disease, trauma, and other social costs.

Exaggerating the good news about moderate drinking, and burying the risks of all drinking, as the headlines, television reports, and "ideal" diets have often done, will have no ameliorative effect on the drinking done by the industry's best customers; it is more likely to help legitimate their unhealthy behavior. Drinkers commonly underestimate their consumption; alcoholics deny that their drinking is a problem and go to great lengths to rationalize their behavior. What could be better than to believe that it's good for you?

We don't live in an ideal world where all drinkers consume moderately. Sadly, we live in a society that's enamored by excess. More is better. People don't like speed limits or restrictions on handguns; they don't respect the limits of their age. They tend to gorge (remember "I can't believe I ate the whole thing"?) and many overdo activities that, in moderation, are clearly good for them, such as taking vitamins or getting some exercise. Let's face it, telling people that alcohol is good for them will not create nirvana.

If the inclusion of moderate drinking in recommendations for a healthy diet would help heavy drinkers reduce their drinking and actually establish mealtime drinking as the norm, I might be less concerned about the societal implications of this marketing strategy. The contrary is more likely to result. Abstainers will take up drinking if they're convinced it's good for them. Current consumers, most of whom drink next to nothing, will begin to drink more.

Yes. The rate of coronary heart disease, and related costs, may drop. On the other hand, we can reasonably predict more alcohol-related problems throughout society as more people drink and consumption rises. Who can say that the pleasure and benefit to drinkers will be worth the car wrecks, family violence, cirrhosis deaths, cancers, crimes and other devastation Americans will suffer? Consider also that, in many cases, innocent third parties, crash victims or family members, and taxpayers, will be the ones hurt.

LIFE-STYLE CHANGES ARE LESS RISKY

We can have a healthier society. But that doesn't necessarily involve encouraging people to drink. Many of the benefits claimed for alcohol are available through life-style changes far less risky than drinking. These include getting regular exercise, avoiding tobacco, eating wisely, and dodging stress. Before we push drinking, we should promote those instead.

In some respects, Americans already get a full dose of messages that link alcohol with health, sexiness, friendships, elegant and relaxed life-styles, and overall well-being. Alcohol promoters have enough marketing tools currently at their disposal to position their products and entice the public to try them. They don't need to promote half truths. Producers and their associates should be required either to tell the whole story about alcohol or cease their efforts to hawk America's costliest drug as the ultimate health potion.

"To fail to inform . . . patients about the benefits of moderate drinking is both counterproductive and dishonest."

DOCTORS SHOULD RECOMMEND ALCOHOL TO THEIR PATIENTS

Stanton Peele

Stanton Peele, a psychologist and researcher, is the author of The Truth About Addiction and Recovery: The Life Process for Outgrowing Destructive Habits and Diseasing of America: How We Allowed Recovery Zealots and the Treatment Industry to Convince Us We Are Out of Control. In the following viewpoint, Peele argues that because moderate drinking is beneficial to human health, doctors should recommend alcohol to their patients. He rejects the argument that providing people with information about alcohol's health benefits will cause them to drink excessively.

As you read, consider the following questions:

1. What are the drawbacks of medications for heart disease, according to the author?
2. In Peele's opinion, at what point do the negative effects of drinking surpass the positive impact?
3. How does the drinking style in "temperance nations" differ from that of wine-drinking nations, as described by Peele?

From Stanton Peele, "Should Physicians Recommend Alcohol to Their Patients? Yes," Priorities, vol. 8, no. 1, 1996. Reprinted with permission from Priorities, a publication of the American Council on Science and Health, 1995 Broadway, 2nd Floor, New York, NY 10023-5860.

Whenever I have visited a physician over the last decade, the following scenario has been replayed: We discuss my cholesterol levels (total, LDL and HDL). We review dietary guidelines and other medical recommendations. Then I say, "Don't forget to remind me to drink a glass or two of wine daily." Invariably, the doctor demurs: "That hasn't been proven to protect you against atherosclerosis."

My doctors, all of whom I have respected and liked, are wrong. Evidence has established beyond question that alcohol reduces coronary artery disease, America's major killer. This result has been found in the Harvard Physician and Nurse studies and in studies by Kaiser Permanente and the American Cancer Society (ACS). Indeed, the evidence that alcohol reduces coronary artery disease and mortality is better than the evidence for the statin drugs, the most potent cholesterol-reducing medications.

Drinking to excess does increase mortality from several sources, such as cancer, cirrhosis and accidents. But a series of studies in the 1990s—including those conducted in conjunction with Kaiser, ACS and Harvard—in the U.S., Britain and Denmark, have found that moderate drinking reduces overall mortality.

A DEMEANING VIEW

Nonetheless, many people object to the idea that doctors should inform their patients that moderate drinking may prolong life. They fear that such advice will justify the excessive drinking some patients already engage in, or they worry that encouragement from doctors will push people who cannot handle alcohol to drink.

The view that people are so stupid or malleable that they will become alcohol abusers because doctors tell them moderate drinking is good for them is demeaning and self-defeating. If people can't regulate their own diets, drinking and exercise, then doctors should avoid giving patients any information about their health behavior, no matter how potentially helpful.

Not only can people handle such information on lifestyle, it offers the primary and best way to attack heart disease. Of course, doctors may also prescribe medications. These medications rarely solve underlying problems, however; and they often cause adverse side effects that counterbalance their positive effects. Because they are not a cure, courses of medication, once begun, are rarely discontinued.

People are the best regulators of their own behaviors. Even those who drink excessively often benefit when doctors provide straightforward, accurate information. Clinical trials conducted by the World Health Organization around the world showed that so-called brief interventions, in which medical personnel advised heavy drinkers to reduce their drinking, are the most successful therapy for problem drinking.

But far more Americans drink less, not more, than would be most healthful for them. To fail to inform these patients about the benefits of moderate drinking is both counterproductive and dishonest. Physicians may ask, "How much alcohol do you drink," "Is there any reason that you don't drink (or that you drink so little)," and (to those without religious objections, previous drinking problems, etc.), "Do you know that one or two glasses of wine or beer a day can be good for your health if you can safely consume them?"

ALCOHOL SUSTAINS LIFE

Here are the data about alcohol and mortality:

1. In 1995 Charles Fuchs and his colleagues at Harvard found that women who drank up to two drinks a day lived longer than abstainers. Subjects were 85,700 nurses.

2. In 1995, Morten Grønbæk and colleagues found that wine drinkers survived longer than abstainers, with those drinking three to five glasses daily having the lowest death rate. Subjects were 20,000 Danes.

3. In 1994, Richard Doll and his colleagues found that men who drank up to two drinks daily lived significantly longer than abstainers. Subjects were 12,300 British doctors.

4. In 1992 Il Suh and colleagues found a 40 percent reduction in coronary mortality among men drinking three and more drinks daily. The 11,700 male subjects were in the upper 10 to 15 percent of risk for coronary heart disease based on their cholesterol, blood pressure and smoking status. Alcohol's enhancement of high density lipoproteins was identified as the protective factor.

5. In 1990, Paolo Boffetta and Lawrence Garfinkel found that men who drank occasionally—up to two drinks daily—outlived abstainers. Subjects were over a quarter of a million volunteers enrolled by the American Cancer Society.

6. In 1990, Arthur Klatsky and his colleagues found that those who drank one or two drinks daily had the lowest overall mortality rate. Subjects were 85,000 Kaiser Permanente patients of both genders and all races.

These data—from large prospective studies of people of both sexes, different occupations, several nations and varying risk profiles—all point to alcohol's life-sustaining effects. This phenomenon is now so well accepted that the U.S. dietary guidelines released in January 1996 recognize that moderate drinking can be beneficial.

BENEFITS VS. RISKS

The levels of drinking at which alcohol lowers death rates are still open to dispute. The new U.S. guidelines indicate that men should not drink more than two drinks per day and women should not exceed one per day. But the British government has set its limits for "sensible drinking" at three to four drinks for men and two to three drinks for women. That abstemiousness increases the risk of death, however, can no longer be doubted. Moreover, alcohol operates at least as effectively as pharmaceuticals to reduce the risk of death for those at high risk for coronary disease.

TABLE 1: TEMPERANCE, ALCOHOL CONSUMPTION, AND CARDIAC MORTALITY

Alcohol Consumption (1990)	Temperance Nations[a]	Non-Temperance Nations[b]
total consumption[c]	6.6	10.8
percent wine	18	44
percent beer	53	40
percent spirits	29	16
AA groups/million population	170	25
coronary mortality[d] (males 50–64)	421	272

[a]Norway, Sweden, U.S., U.K., Ireland, Australia, New Zealand, Canada, Finland, Iceland

[b]Italy, France, Spain, Portugal, Switzerland, Germany, Denmark, Austria, Belgium, Luxembourg, Netherlands

[c]Liters consumed per capita per year

[d]Deaths per 100,000 population

Source: Stanton Peele, *Culture, Alcohol, and Health: The Consequences of Alcohol Consumption Among Western Nations*, December 1, 1995.

At one point, researchers questioned whether people who had quit drinking due to previous health problems inflated the mortality rate among abstainers. But this position can no longer be maintained. The studies described above separated drinkers who had quit drinking and who had preexisting health problems from other nondrinkers. The benefits of drinking persisted with these individuals omitted.

At some point, ranging from three to six drinks daily, the negative effects of drinking for cancer, cirrhosis and accidents catch up to and surpass alcohol's beneficial cardiac impact. Moreover, women under 50—who have relatively low rates of heart disease and relatively high rates of breast cancer mortality—may not benefit from drinking.

That is, unless they have one or more cardiac risk factors. Even younger women with such risk factors benefit from light to moderate drinking. And, we must remember, most American women and men have such risk factors. (Fuchs et al. found about three quarters of the nurses in the Harvard study had at least one.) Remember, over all ages, American women are ten times as likely to die of heart disease (40 percent) as of breast cancer (4 percent).

TEMPERANCE NATIONS HAVE MORE DRINKING PROBLEMS

Why, then, do Americans—physicians, public health workers, educators and political leaders— refuse to recognize alcohol's benefits? We might also ask why the United States banned the manufacture, sale and transportation of alcoholic beverages from 1920 to 1933. It is probably too obvious to mention that alcohol has never been banned—or prohibition even seriously discussed— in France, Italy, Spain and a number of other European nations.

What is it about America and some other nations that prevents them from considering that alcohol may be good for people? These so-called "temperance" nations see alcohol in a highly negative light. This is true even though nations with higher alcohol consumption have lower death rates from coronary heart disease (see Table 1). Oddly, temperance nations—despite concentrating on alcohol problem prevention and treatment—actually have more drinking problems than those in which alcohol is socially accepted and integrated.

This occurs even though temperance nations drink less alcohol. But they drink a higher percentage of their alcohol in the form of spirits. This drinking is more likely to take place in concentrated bursts among men at sporting events or in drinking establishments. This style of drinking contrasts with that in wine-drinking nations, which encourage socialized drinking among family members of both genders and all ages at meals and other social gatherings. These cultures do not teach people that alcohol is an addictive drug. Rather, moderate drinking is modeled for children and taught to them in the home. Furthermore, these cultures accept that drinking may be good for you. We should, too.

| "Encouraging drinking for any reason is a risky business."

DOCTORS SHOULD NOT RECOMMEND ALCOHOL TO THEIR PATIENTS

Michael H. Criqui

Michael H. Criqui is a professor in the Departments of Medicine and Family and Preventive Medicine at the University of California, San Diego. In the following viewpoint, Criqui maintains that although moderate drinking helps to prevent cardiovascular disease, doctors should not recommend alcohol to their patients. He contends that the risk of alcoholism and of adverse health effects due to heavy drinking outweigh the benefits derived from moderate drinking. Nondrinkers should not be advised to start drinking, he concludes, and light drinkers should not be encouraged to drink more.

As you read, consider the following questions:

1. What percentage of drinkers are alcoholics, according to Criqui?
2. According to the author, what is the relationship between a society's enthusiasm for alcohol consumption and its levels of alcohol abuse?
3. In the Canadian study described by Criqui, what alcohol-related causes of death resulted in potential years of life lost?

From Michael H. Criqui, "Moderate Drinking: Benefits and Risks," chapter 7 of *Alcohol and the Cardiovascular System*, edited by Sam Zakhari and Momtaz Wassef, National Institute on Alcohol Abuse and Alcoholism Research Monograph 31 (Washington, DC: U.S. Dept. of Health & Human Services, 1996). (Notes/references in the original have been omitted here.)

Nonmoderate drinking, defined as more than 2 drinks per day, is associated with an increased risk of cardiovascular disease (CVD) as well as non-CVD conditions and an increase in total morbidity and mortality. However, lighter (moderate) drinking, defined as 2 standard-size drinks per day or less, is associated with a reduced rate of ischemic CVD events, most specifically coronary heart disease. In addition, at 2 or less standard-size drinks per day, in general there is little increase in the risk of non-CVD conditions, with the probable exception of breast cancer. The risk of breast cancer appears to increase linearly at about 10 percent per drink per day. Although the data are less consistent, the risk of colon cancer may also be somewhat increased, even at moderate levels of alcohol consumption.

DO THE BENEFITS EXCEED THE RISKS?

Let us assume for a moment that "moderate drinker" is a stable classification—that is, that the moderate drinker never exceeds 2 standard drinks per day. It is unclear how many persons fit this classification and thus can be considered true moderate drinkers. The exact proportion cannot be accurately determined by epidemiological studies that have typically addressed "usual consumption" or "consumption in the previous week."

Several factors must be taken into account when determining the risk/benefit ratio for true moderate drinkers. First, how old is the drinker in question? Clearly, younger persons cannot possibly benefit much from alcohol consumption, at least in the short term, because their risk of ischemic CVD events is low. In fact, in a study of 128,934 participants in a prepaid health plan, the overall reduction in mortality in moderate drinkers was limited to those 60 years of age and older.

Second, is the drinker in question otherwise at increased risk of ischemic CVD? Moderate drinkers with no family history of CVD and no other CVD risk factors are unlikely to receive much benefit from drinking, because their risk is already low. This assumption has been confirmed in the British Regional Heart Study, where broad exclusions for CVD risk in men produced a very low risk for CVD events and a predictable nonassociation with alcohol. Similarly, a 1995 study of U.S. nurses revealed the benefits to be clearly evident only in women at increased risk of CVD.

Third, is the drinker in question otherwise at increased risk of hemorrhagic CVD or non-CVD events? Extensive research on the biological pathways for alcohol's effect on ischemic events indicates major protective effects for ischemic CVD events through high-density lipoprotein (HDL) cholesterol and through reduced coagulation. Someone with already reduced coagulation (e.g., from aspirin therapy or a low fibrinogen) could be at increased risk for hemorrhagic events, including hemorrhagic stroke, from even moderate alcohol consumption.

THE PATIENT MUST DECIDE

We conclude that the regular consumption of relatively large amounts of alcohol—that is, three or more drinks per day—is undesirable from the standpoint of health for almost all people and that drinking low-to-moderate amounts can be desirable or undesirable, depending on individual characteristics. . . .

Currently, indiscriminate advice to nondrinkers to take up alcohol for health reasons is inappropriate, but some people (e.g., those at high risk for coronary heart disease but low risk for problem drinking) may benefit. Risks to health must also be weighed against the non–health-related benefits of alcohol. As in other areas of health care, the patient must, with our guidance, make the final decision.

Gary D. Friedman and Arthur L. Klatsky, *New England Journal of Medicine*, December 16, 1993.

Fourth, does the drinker in question have, for other reasons, an elevated risk of colon cancer, or breast cancer if the drinker is a woman? For example, is there a family history of these diseases? If so, potential CVD benefit may be particularly problematic.

Fifth, is the drinker in question unusually or capriciously susceptible to the intoxicating effects of even moderate amounts of alcohol? If so, moderate drinking could pose a significant hazard.

In summary, there are moderate drinkers who could show overall benefits for ischemic CVD events that exceed risks from other causes. However, for the reasons outlined above, the risk/benefit ratio in some moderate drinkers may not be favorable.

DOCTORS SHOULD NOT RECOMMEND MODERATE DRINKING

The preceding section addressed the true moderate drinker. Unfortunately, not everyone can drink moderately, even if they so wish. Several issues require consideration.

First, would it be wise to encourage nondrinkers to begin drinking to reduce the risk of ischemic CVD? In the United States currently about 75 percent of adults drink some alcohol. Half of all drinkers have had at least temporary problems with alcohol. For between 5 and 10 percent of drinkers, the problems are profound—that is, they are alcoholics. Thus, encouraging drinking for any reason is a risky business.

Second, who are the nondrinkers? They include persons with any of the following characteristics: a personal history of alcoholism, a family history of alcoholism, a personal dislike for the intoxicating effects of alcohol, a personal dislike for the taste of alcohol, and religious or ethical objections to the consumption of alcohol. It would appear unwise to attempt to achieve a reduction in ischemic CVD risk by encouraging any level of alcohol consumption in nondrinkers.

Third, should light drinkers (less than or 1 drink per day) be encouraged to drink more? Alcohol may still have a benefit for ischemic CVD events at levels as high as 5 drinks per day, which answers the question of how much you can drink and still get benefit for ischemic CVD events. Five drinks a day, however, would result in a considerable increase in overall morbidity and mortality. A much better question is, if one wants the benefit for ischemic CVD events, how little can one drink and still get the maximum benefit? The surprising answer is perhaps a little less than 1 drink per day. Thus, many light drinkers are achieving nearly all the benefit, with little risk of harm. In addition, some light drinkers may be deliberately limiting their consumption because of previous problems in controlling their alcohol intake, and they clearly should not be encouraged to drink more.

In summary, many people have problems with alcohol. Those without alcohol problems drink moderately and responsibly, or they do not drink at all. The nondrinking group includes very few individuals for whom it would be appropriate to encourage drinking for CVD benefit.

INSIGHTS FROM STUDIES

Ecological studies provide insight into the benefits versus the risks of alcohol consumption in large populations. Countries with heavy consumption of alcohol, mostly wine-drinking countries, show reduced coronary death rates. However, even though this analysis was restricted to ages 35–74 years, in which coronary disease is common, there was no increase in longevity. This reflects the robust association between the average consumption of alcohol in a society and the proportion of heavy drinkers. . . . Thus, overall enthusiasm for alcohol consumption in a society is closely paralleled by higher levels of abuse.

Perhaps the largest epidemiological study ever to evaluate the relationship between alcohol consumption and mortality was the American Cancer Society prospective study of 276,802 men aged 40–59 at baseline in the year 1959. The results for men are quite representative of the usual finding in epidemiological studies. There was a benefit for coronary heart disease, but this benefit was optimal at 1 drink per day; that is, no additional benefit was attained at higher levels of alcohol consumption. In addition, at 1 drink per day, there was no evidence of an increase in non-CVD endpoints. However, beginning at 2 drinks per day, there was a steady increase in the risk of cerebrovascular diseases, cancer, accidents and violence, and all-cause mortality. These data clearly indicate, in a very large data set, the overall risk/benefit ratio for each mortality endpoint at each level of alcohol consumption, and illustrate that an overall (all-cause mortality) benefit is restricted to quite moderate drinking.

POTENTIAL YEARS OF LIFE LOST

Epidemiological studies generally allow inferences to be drawn about the age-specific risks of death from various causes. Most epidemiological studies of CVD have focused on middle-aged or elderly groups. . . . Such studies tend to overlook the simple fact that study participation is predicated on survival to the minimum age for study inclusion.

Perhaps a more useful way to evaluate total risk is to consider potential years of life lost (PYLL) from various conditions before an arbitrary older age (e.g., 75). Data from Canada for PYLL in men in 1990 [show that] although coronary disease ranks first in PYLL, it is followed closely by motor vehicle crashes and then suicide, both of which are associated with alcohol consumption and which together are associated with about 50 percent more PYLL than coronary disease. Other alcohol-linked causes of death also make large contributions to PYLL in men, such as HIV infection, stroke, cancer of the large intestine, cirrhosis, and homicide. Data from Canada for PYLL in women [show that] both breast cancer and motor vehicle crashes individually contribute more PYLL than coronary disease; suicide, stroke, cancer of the large intestine, homicide, and cirrhosis contribute substantial PYLL in women as well. In the United States in 1990, it was estimated that alcohol caused over 100,000 deaths.

NOT A GOOD IDEA

It seems reasonable that selected patients at elevated risk of ischemic CVD events who are known to use and to have used alcohol responsibly should discuss the risks and benefits of alcohol consumption with their physicians. Such patients can be counseled based on their individual situation.

Any more general recommendation is equivalent to recommending alcohol for use as a pharmacological agent for protection from ischemic CVD events. Is this a good idea? If alcohol were proposed as a new pharmaceutical for the prevention of ischemic CVD events, Food and Drug Administration–required clinical trials in human subjects would reveal a dose-related suppression of cognitive and motor abilities in all subjects, with about 10 percent of subjects developing addiction and alcoholism. In addition, comprehensive clinical reports would indicate that the consequences of alcoholism extended to friends and relatives of the subjects, and frequently even strangers. After weighing the risks and benefits of such a drug, the FDA clearly could not approve it for general use for CVD protection. Similarly, we should not routinely recommend alcohol for CVD protection.

PERIODICAL BIBLIOGRAPHY

The following articles have been selected to supplement the diverse views presented in this chapter. Addresses are provided for periodicals not indexed in the *Readers' Guide to Periodical Literature*, the *Alternative Press Index*, the *Social Sciences Index*, or the *Index to Legal Periodicals and Books*.

David U. Andrews	"Tempest in a Six-Pack," *In These Times*, February 20–March 5, 1995.
John Berlau	"Drink to Your Heart's Content?" *Insight*, March 3, 1997. Available from 3600 New York Ave. NE, Washington, DC 20002.
Carey Burkett	"All Things in Moderation," *Sojourners*, December 1994/January 1995.
Marian Burros	"In an About-Face, U.S. Says Alcohol Has Health Benefits," *New York Times*, January 3, 1996.
Stephen Chapman	"Is an Ignorant Consumer a Safe Consumer?" *Conservative Chronicle*, February 14, 1996. Available from Box 37077, Boone, IA 50037-0077.
Marilyn Chase	"Beneficial Drinking: After Abstinence, Before Tying One On," *Wall Street Journal*, July 3, 1995.
Gary D. Friedman and Arthur L. Klatsky	"Is Alcohol Good for Your Health?" *New England Journal of Medicine*, December 16, 1993. Available from 10 Shattuck St., Boston, MA 02115-6094.
William Grimes	"Good News on Drinking; Fries with That, Please," *New York Times*, January 7, 1996.
John Hinman and Michael Criqui	"Should Wine Bottles and Liquor Labels Be Allowed to Carry Health Claims?" *Health*, May/June 1996.
Suzanne Jennings	"Wishful Thinking," *Forbes*, September 13, 1993.
Maria Piombo and Melinda Piles	"The Relationship Between College Females' Drinking and Their Sexual Behaviors," *Women's Health Issues*, July/August 1996. Available from Elsevier Science, Inc., 655 Avenue of the Americas, New York, NY 10010.
Ben Sherwood	"Wine and Poses," *Washington Monthly*, May 1993.
Jacob Sullum	"B.A.T.F. Out of Hell," *Reason*, May 1994.

DOES THE ALCOHOL INDUSTRY MARKET ITS PRODUCTS RESPONSIBLY?

CHAPTER PREFACE

In June 1996, a Corpus Christi, Texas, television station aired an advertisement that featured two dogs on a stage. The first dog, identified as an "obedience school graduate," carried a newspaper in its mouth. The second dog, identified as "valedictorian," carried a purple velvet bag containing a bottle of Seagram's Royal Crown whiskey.

This ad was not remarkable for its content; it was remarkable because it signaled the end of the liquor industry's self-imposed ban on television advertising. Several months later, in November 1996, came the official announcement: The distilled spirits industry—the producers of hard liquors such as whiskey, vodka, and gin—would lift its voluntary bans on radio and television ads, which had been in effect since 1936 and 1948, respectively.

This announcement provoked intense criticism from many media commentators, politicians, and public health officials. President Bill Clinton called the move "irresponsible" and condemned the industry for "exposing our children to such ads before they know how to handle alcohol or are legally allowed to do so." Clinton and other critics fear that the ads will lead to an increase in alcohol consumption and alcohol-related problems—such as alcohol abuse and drunk driving—among children and teenagers.

The liquor industry has defended its decision to air TV and radio ads on several grounds. Fred A. Meister, the president and CEO of the Distilled Spirits Council of the United States (DISCUS), points out that the ban had been voluntary. He argues that the liquor industry has the same legal right to advertise as do beer and wine producers, who have a long tradition of advertising on TV and radio. Meister and others also reject the argument that such advertising will cause an increase in alcohol abuse among young people. According to Morris E. Chafetz, president of the Health Education Foundation, "There is not a single study . . . that credibly connects advertising with an increase in alcohol use or abuse." Therefore, supporters of the ads maintain, the liquor industry is not being irresponsible by lifting the ban.

The controversy over the effects of liquor advertising is just one of the issues debated in the following chapter on whether the alcohol industry markets its products in a responsible manner.

| *"Ads for hard liquor . . . should have
| no place on television or radio."*

ADVERTISING LIQUOR ON TELEVISION AND RADIO IS IRRESPONSIBLE

Part I: American Medical Association, Part II: John Hughes

In November 1996, the distilled beverage industry discontinued its self-imposed ban on television and radio liquor advertisements. In the following two-part viewpoint, the American Medical Association (AMA) and John Hughes assert that the industry's decision to begin airing ads is irresponsible. In Part I, the AMA argues that public pressure should be brought to bear on the industry in order to prevent hard liquor ads from running on television and radio. In Part II, John Hughes maintains that by airing such ads, the liquor industry hopes to "hook a new generation" on alcohol. He contends that this decision could exacerbate alcohol-related problems, including drunk driving and binge drinking among college students. The AMA is America's primary professional association for physicians. John Hughes is a professor of journalism and the director of the International Media Studies Program at Brigham Young University in Provo, Utah.

As you read, consider the following questions:

1. What "legitimate public health message" is the liquor industry distorting, according to the AMA?
2. How much money per year does the distilled spirits industry spend on advertising, as reported by Hughes? How much do beer and wine manufacturers spend?
3. How have some colleges responded to the problem of alcohol abuse among students, according to Hughes?

(Part I) American Medical Association, "Responsibility on the Rocks," *American Medical News*, December 16, 1996, p. 15. Copyright 1996, American Medical Association. Reprinted with permission. (Part II) John Hughes, "Stop New Liquor Ads Before They Start," *Christian Science Monitor*, November 13, 1996. Reprinted by permission of the author.

I

The question of whether ads for hard liquor should be broadcast has prompted two vastly different displays of corporate responsibility.

The first, a dismal one, comes from the hard liquor industry, the makers of whiskey, gin, vodka and the like. In November 1995, that industry's trade group, the Distilled Spirits Council of the United States, decided to drop its voluntary, nearly 50-year ban on television ads. The council followed the lead of distiller Joseph Seagram & Sons, which unilaterally broke the ban by placing a whiskey ad on a Texas television station in June.

The second, a much more positive response, comes from the major television networks—ABC, CBS, NBC and Fox. All have wisely decided to reject the ads.

Problem solved? Not quite.

While the broadcast networks have decided to hold the line—at least for now—cable channels and local television and radio stations are not bound by the decision. Some hard liquor ads have already started popping up, and more are expected.

The Wrong Direction

This is absolutely the wrong direction to go. Ads for hard liquor—and in the AMA's opinion, any alcohol product—should have no place on television or radio.

The position of the distillers is that their message is aimed at adults. But television, as we all know, sends its messages out indiscriminately to young and old alike.

This comes at a time when there is already a major problem with young people and alcohol. An AMA-sponsored study early in 1996 found that one in five Americans 18 to 30 admit to being binge drinkers. Among 18-year-olds in the same survey, 22% admitted that on an average night of drinking they downed four or more drinks. Other research has found that 87% of high school students have experimented with alcohol.

Market analysts say the hard liquor ads are a strategic response to the fact that hard liquor consumption has dropped dramatically—nearing 30% in the past decade and a half. (That in itself should be celebrated as a public health victory.) Distillers appear to be taking a lesson from the beer business, which spends $600 million a year on television ads and has avoided a similar drop.

And while we're on the subject of beer advertising, it's hard to believe that the brewers will quietly give up their market share. The last thing we need is an advertising and marketing "arms race" among alcohol companies. America's young people would surely be the losers.

Twisting the Message

What's also very troubling is that, to make their case, the distillers are twisting a legitimate public health message. Warnings, ironically about drunk driving, have long made the point that in terms of alcohol content, a stein of beer is a glass of wine is a shot of whiskey. So, the distillers reason, why should they be singled out?

Unfortunately, when young people are part of the scenario, the risk is too great that their lack of judgment will extend to the quantity of hard liquor they drink. In this instance, trying to equate different types of alcohol sends the wrong message.

President Bill Clinton has condemned the hard liquor ads as irresponsible. Federal Communications Commission Chairman Reed Hundt has also expressed reservations about the ads, and his staff is studying the issue.

The AMA has already gone on record against the ads. You can make your voice heard too. Call and protest when you encounter hard liquor ads on cable, local television and radio. Most importantly, the FCC should hear the concerns of physicians about these ads. . . .

If the hard liquor industry can't make up its mind to act responsibly, the FCC should make the decision for it.

II

Twenty or 30 years ago, novels and movies depicted journalists as a hard-drinking bunch.

As a nondrinker myself, I wasn't caused any career problems by my colleagues who drank, but I noted that overindulgence in liquor caused a fair amount of misery, family breakups, professional disaster, and, in a few cases, self-destruction.

Today, journalism is a much more sober profession. Journalists are more likely to drink less alcohol, and often none at all.

In part that is a reflection of trends in society in general. While there is still a great deal of experimentation with alcohol at the high school and college level, many more, mature citizens have become better educated about its effect on their health, safety, and general well-being.

Why, then, is the liquor industry trying to turn the clock back? For some months, marketers of distilled spirits have been experimenting with a return of radio and television advertising of their products after a long voluntary ban. In the case of radio advertising, the ban dates back to 1936, and to 1948 in the case of television. Now the marketers of vodka, whiskey, gin, rum, and other hard liquors have gone public with their plan to boost sales through television advertising. . . .

A RESPONSIBLE DECISION?

Already the distilled spirits industry spends more than $230 million a year on advertising, most of it for print and outdoor billboards. But the industry covets the audience in its early 20s that is presently being wooed on television by the beer and wine manufacturers with about $700 million a year in advertising.

The aim of the new advertising plan is to hook a new generation on a product that clearly has an impact on the rate of drunk driving incidents and other community problems. The distilled-spirits industry responds with the argument that its advertising will be "responsible."

A lot of critics don't buy that. Neither does President Clinton. In a weekend radio address he blasted the plan for expanded liquor advertising as "irresponsible." By introducing the ads, the president said, the liquor industry will be "exposing our children to such ads before they know how to handle alcohol or are legally allowed to do so."

ADVERTISING AND BRAND AWARENESS AMONG CHILDREN

A study by the Berkeley, Calif.-based Center on Alcohol Advertising found advertising enhances children's brand awareness— representing about 20 percent of the way kids decide what they will drink.

In the spring of 1996, the center did a survey of kids age 9 to 11 that found Anheuser-Busch's animated Budweiser frogs were more recognized than Smokey the Bear or Tony the Tiger.

Only Bugs Bunny had better recognition among well-known cartoon characters.

Ron Scherer and Nicole Gaouette, *Christian Science Monitor*, December 26, 1996.

The major television networks are skittish about accepting the new hard liquor ads. They understand, and fear, the reaction of parents and organized antiliquor groups. But the networks no longer control the market. With the explosion of new technology, there are hundreds of independent radio and television stations, along with computer and cable outlets.

Their reaction to the new advertising campaign should be

carefully monitored. If they air it, viewers should protest. Alcohol use, abuse, and addiction is one of the most serious problems confronting our society today. Nobody in search of a bigger dollar profit margin should be allowed to inject a new generation of Americans into the problem with image-advertising depicting hard liquor use as "cool."

Ironically, the new advertising is intended to debut at a time when there is substantial debate on college campuses about the use and impact of alcohol. The Commission on Substance Abuse at Colleges and Universities reported in 1995 that 95 percent of violent crimes on campuses, as well as 40 percent of academic problems, are alcohol-related.

At the University of Notre Dame, whose president headed the commission, the campus daily newspaper polled students and discovered that 72 percent were regular drinkers, with 49 percent getting drunk twice a week.

SCHOOLS DEAL WITH ALCOHOL

But some other universities that previously permitted alcohol on campus have banned it. At some, such as the University of Colorado, fraternities and sororities have voted to ban alcohol from gatherings held in chapter houses. Some students on campuses where alcohol is permitted have elected to have alcohol-free dormitories for nondrinkers.

As David Hoekema, academic dean at Calvin College in Grand Rapids, Mich., wrote in a letter to the New York Times, we cannot "abdicate all responsibility for students' moral life. Both faculty and student-life staff members have a duty to help young adults understand what it means to make responsible choices."

The most effective cutbacks in college-age alcohol use take place when students themselves take the initiative, rather than responding to administration-imposed bans. But resisting the college binge-drinking culture requires some maturity on the part of teenagers and early 20-year-olds. They don't need to be undermined by liquor dealers in search of higher profits at society's expense.

"Society can observe and even enjoy
alcohol advertising on radio and
television and make appropriate
choices."

ADVERTISING LIQUOR ON TELEVISION AND RADIO IS NOT IRRESPONSIBLE

Fred A. Meister

Fred A. Meister is the president and CEO of the Distilled Spirits
Council of the United States (DISCUS), a trade association that
represents the distilled spirits industry. In the following viewpoint, Meister defends the distilled spirits industry's decision to
end its self-imposed ban on television and radio liquor ads. Rejecting the commonly held view that alcohol advertising contributes to the problem of alcohol abuse by young people, he
insists that the distilled spirits industry has a First Amendment
right to advertise its products. Distilled spirits are equivalent to
beer and wine, according to Meister, so the liquor industry
should have the same freedom to advertise that beer and wine
producers enjoy.

As you read, consider the following questions:

1. How has television changed, according to Meister?
2. What evidence does the author give to support his
   contention that underage drinking has declined?
3. How did the readers of the *Washington Post* respond to the
   newspaper's question regarding alcohol advertising on
   television, as quoted by Meister?

From "Alcohol Advertising on Television," a position paper of the Distilled Spirits
Council of the United States (DISCUS) adapted from a speech by Fred A. Meister,
delivered December 10, 1996, to the Media Institute, Washington, D.C. Reprinted by
permission of DISCUS.

L iquor ads have now joined the variety of alcohol ads that have appeared on television and radio for decades. So now, and in the future, you will see and hear on television and radio some liquor ads. They likely will be few in number compared to advertising by the other forms of alcohol—beer and wine. There is roughly $675 million each year of beer and wine advertising on television and radio.

Beer and wine have been on television for decades and there has rightly been no great public outcry or controversy. Just because another form of alcohol—distilled spirits—is advertising, there is no reason for public outcry or controversy. Not only is alcohol advertising a legal right, but it has been and is socially acceptable to society. Nothing has changed, nor should it.

THE CHANGING MEDIA LANDSCAPE

Should the distilled spirits industry have continued their voluntary decision to refrain from advertising—a decision based on a medium that is vastly different today than 48 years ago? Obviously, the answer is no.

Television today is dramatically different and will continue to change in the days and years to come. When spirits initially refrained from broadcasting ads, the television industry was characterized by few channels to choose from and, at most, one television in every home. The industry chose to forego its prerogative to use it and in retrospect it has paid dearly for that decision. It brings to mind the old refrain that no good deed goes unpunished. The fact is, however, that choosing not to exercise one's First Amendment rights does not mean those rights expire.

Today, television can be used to direct advertising messages to adults in the same way that alcohol advertisers use other forms of media to reach adult audiences.

Now, the majority of homes have 2, 3 or 4 televisions. There is satellite TV as well as combination TV-computers with interactive links through phone-lines. Our information options are exploding. The lines between print, broadcast, cable and computer are being blurred more everyday. We now have multi-media potential to transmit voice and video where only data has gone before. And at the center of all of it is—the box. The TV is the point of entry; the pipeline into the information-rich environment of now and the future.

Distilled spirit companies want to access responsibly those 100 million adults who drink beverage alcohol, just as do beer and wine companies. We want to provide those 100 million adult consumers with the same product information for our fine brands as they now receive for beer and wine. Make no mistake about it. Beer drinkers are also spirits drinkers, wine drinkers are spirits drinkers. We need to compete in the marketplace by educating and informing these adult consumers about our products through our ads.

UNDERAGE DRINKING HAS DECLINED

Should we in the distilled spirits industry not advertise because the society is in the midst of some sort of crisis regarding reckless behavior associated with alcohol? No, the fact is that the trends are just the reverse.

While beer television/cable advertising has increased from over $300 million in 1980 to over $600 million today, we've seen a decline in the key indicators for underage drinking:

• According to the Federal government's survey of youth and alcohol use, since 1979 the percentage of 12 to 17 year olds who have ever taken a drink has declined by 46%.

• In the past 15 years, binge drinking among high school seniors is down 28%.

• And during that time, fatal auto accidents involving teenage drunk drivers is down 68%.

In the words of the government's traffic authority, the U.S. Department of Transportation's National Highway Traffic Safety Administration (NHTSA):

> The national effort to reduce motor vehicle deaths and injuries of young people between ages 15 and 20 has been a success story. Although far too many youth still die tragically in these crashes, fatality reductions over the past decade, especially those that are alcohol related, have been remarkable.

We fully agree with that statement.

The national media reported that the number of fatal alcohol related auto crashes had a slight increase for the first time in many years. This slight increase after a steady downward trend since 1982 could be attributed to many factors. After all, speed limits are going up, the number of kids driving is going up, the number of cars they have is going up, and the number of hours they spend behind the wheel is going up. In the face of all those trends, it is encouraging that there is every evidence that irresponsible drinking overall is on the decline.

A troubling aspect of the issue of alcohol and young people is the too often used phrase *"alcohol and other drugs."* Many children go home to parents who drink alcohol on a reasonable, regular basis. After all, there are 100 million adult drinkers in America. Then these children hear the message that alcohol and illegal drugs are somehow similar, if not identical. Well, if your parents are drinking distilled spirits, or beer or wine, and the banner in school draws a parallel between alcohol and pot, what is the kid led to believe about pot? The answer, seemingly quite vividly, was reported in the December 9, 1996, issue of *Time* magazine about students at the prominent Chicago suburban high school, New Trier.

According to the article, "For most, marijuana is an ancillary pleasure of growing up comfortably in the 90's, not the least bit incompatible with varsity athletics, the spring musical or advanced-placement chemistry. . . . The very ordinariness of drug use leads some to conclude that it is without risk."

With regard to alcohol advertising, those who try on the one hand to distinguish spirits from beer and wine or on the other hand to attach any form of alcohol to illegal drugs are doing a disservice to our children.

PART OF A NORMAL ADULT LIFESTYLE

Alcohol, be it distilled, brewed or vinted, is a beverage that is a perfectly appropriate part of the enjoyment of a responsible adult lifestyle. There is nothing wrong with responsible drinking, for those adults who choose that particular pleasure.

The goal of our advertising is to offer our brands—if you will, our tastes and flavors—to the range of options known to those adults who choose to drink. It is as simple as that.

This point is distinctly different from the issues associated with tobacco. It is increasingly apparent with every passing day that the public is told that it should not smoke. This is quite different from the public's attitude towards drinking. When it comes to beer, wine and spirits, the public is told that it is important for every adult who chooses to drink, to do so responsibly. The spirits industry always has made responsible drinking by adults a cornerstone of its business.

The distilled spirits industry has been a longtime and fully committed participant in efforts promoting alcohol education, meaningful and effective drunk driving laws, strict enforcement and treatment. DISCUS' members have been part of industry-wide efforts, such as the Century Council, to combat drunk driving and underage drinking. We've also supported dozens and dozens of other campaigns, including the nationally known "Cops in Shops" and "Friends Don't Let Friends Drive Drunk."

Over two years ago, DISCUS crafted, introduced and continues to lobby in state capitals for model legislation we call the Drunk Driving Prevention Act—a blueprint for aggressive state action to curb alcohol abuse and any underage use. Our legislation eliminates any gray area. We call for zero tolerance, automatic—not optional—license revocation, a ban on open alcohol containers in autos, mandatory alcohol education for new drivers and mandatory drug and alcohol testing in fatal crashes. To date, 13 states have adopted all or part of our proposal.

SPIRITS ADVERTISING MEETS OR EXCEEDS STANDARDS

To return to the fundamental question, why shouldn't spirits advertise on television? Does it impose an unreasonable risk to our children? No. Society has accepted each year almost three-quarters of a billion dollars of electronic advertising for beer and wine. There is no basis to arbitrarily draw the line at our entry. Those industries have set the standard for alcohol advertising and the public seems comfortable with that standard. We emphatically support the right of beer and wine to advertise on television. Alcohol, in whatever form, is a legal product and should be advertised on television.

While the current Federal Communications Commission (FCC) Chairman may have forgotten about the First Amendment, several of his colleagues, the Congress and the Courts are appropriately sensitive to the vitally important First Amendment Rights of broadcasters and responsible advertisers.

If, however, the public should say that it wants to discuss those standards for all forms of alcohol, that is fine. We are fully cognizant of the standards set and we are completely comfortable that we will meet and exceed them.

ALCOHOL EQUIVALENCE

Typical servings of beer, wine and spirits all contain roughly the same amount of alcohol. And the alcohol in any form has the same effect on the body. This is why so many agencies of government, from dozens of driver's manuals to Federal Departments, and Mothers Against Drunk Driving teach what is known as the fact of alcohol equivalence. That is, in terms of the way most people drink beverage alcohol, a 12 ounce bottle of beer, a five ounce glass of wine, or a cocktail containing one and one-half ounces of distilled spirits all contain the same amount of alcohol.

Government and private sector groups are not teaching alcohol equivalence for our sake. They are teaching it because it is important that people know what they are drinking. Knowing about the alcohol in a typical serving of beer, wine and distilled spirits is a critical aspect of responsible drinking, and clearly responsible drinking is what society wants to see. Alcohol of any type can be used responsibly—alcohol of any type can be abused. There is a practice of moderation, never a drink of moderation.

Look at law enforcement. Blood alcohol content is the standard measure for driving under the influence, as it should be. To a breathalyzer, and the police officer, all alcohol is the same; whether it's in someone's system through a cocktail or a can of beer simply doesn't matter.

RESPONSIBLE PROMOTION

Distilled spirits advertising and marketing materials should portray distilled spirits and drinkers in a responsible manner. These materials should not show a distilled spirits product being consumed abusively or irresponsibly.

Distilled spirits advertising and marketing materials should not promote the intoxicating effects of beverage alcohol consumption.

Distilled spirits advertising and marketing materials should contain no claims or representations that individuals can obtain social, professional, educational, or athletic success or status as a result of beverage alcohol consumption.

Distilled Spirits Council of the United States, Code of Good Practice for Distilled Spirits Advertising and Marketing, 1996.

Too many Americans don't understand the fundamental similarities among beverage alcohol types. Some policy-makers make distinctions that discriminate against spirits and favor beer and wine because of a misunderstanding of the fundamental facts regarding alcohol.

There is no reason to ask the spirits industry not to advertise on television when no one is asking its competitors to do likewise. And, importantly, no one should ask our competitors to volunteer for such restraint. Decades of experience tell us that this society can observe and even enjoy alcohol advertising on radio and television and make appropriate choices.

ADVERTISING DOES NOT CAUSE CONSUMPTION OR ABUSE

Simply put, advertising does not cause an individual to begin drinking or to abuse alcohol. Our own government's studies and statements confirm these facts:

- "Research has yet to document a strong relationship between alcohol advertising and alcohol consumption."—1990 Department of Health and Human Services report to Congress
- "No reliable basis on which to conclude that alcohol advertising significantly affects alcohol abuse. Absent such evidence,

there is no basis for concluding that rules banning or otherwise limiting alcohol advertising would offer significant protection to the public."—1985 conclusion of the Federal Trade Commission study on alcohol advertising. . . .

AMERICANS ACCEPT RESPONSIBLE ALCOHOL ADVERTISING

According to a survey in *Advertising Age* regarding some of the markets (or television stations) where spirits advertising has appeared, "the spots haven't drawn a single complaint."

There have also been a number of positive editorials and commentaries recognizing that spirits advertising is just another form of alcohol advertising that they have been seeing for decades. The *Washington Post* printed a notice asking readers to write in and answer the question, "Does liquor advertising belong on television?" Several weeks later, this was the paper's conclusion:

> Our correspondents, although not large in volume, had strong views on this topic. Most argued that if beer and wine ads were permissible, it would be inconsistent not to allow liquor ads as well. A government imposed ban on all alcohol ads drew almost no takers. Those worried about the effect of advertising on children preferred parents as regulators over the Federal Communications Commission. Warning to Madison Avenue: Some writers didn't think advertising has as much impact on viewers as you do.

Also, according to our polls, anywhere from 30 to 50 percent of the public thought that we had been advertising on television for years, so what's the issue now?

What about Talk Radio—that great barometer of public debate? According to *Talkers Magazine*, the "bible" of talk radio, liquor ads on television aren't even on the top 10 list of hot topics of what callers want to talk about. In short, people understand that alcohol advertising is not a new, or even an interesting subject, since they have seen it for decades.

RESPONSIBILITY IS REQUIRED BY ALL

In advertising, as in every other aspect of our business operations, we are very cognizant of our role of responsibility. We ask for a commensurate commitment to responsibility in the words and actions of those who are speaking out in this environment.

If we all take care to consider the facts, to respect the freedoms and responsibilities of the government, the media and the beverage alcohol industry, television alcohol advertising will be just as acceptable and appropriate next year as it has been in the past.

The fact that the spirits industry has joined the mix should not, and we believe will not, change that fundamental acceptance.

> "In dropping their self-imposed ban on TV ads, the distillers said they wouldn't target the young. We should be dubious."

TELEVISION LIQUOR ADS MAY PROMOTE UNDERAGE DRINKING

John Leo

In the following viewpoint, John Leo criticizes the liquor industry's decision to end its self-imposed ban on television liquor ads. Leo argues that with the ban lifted, the industry is likely to produce advertisements designed to lure young people to drink hard liquor. Such ads, he asserts, will result in more drinking, addiction, and drunk driving among the young. Leo concludes that both beer and liquor ads should be regulated in order to minimize their destructive consequences. Leo is a syndicated columnist and a contributing editor for *U.S. News & World Report*, a national weekly newsmagazine.

As you read, consider the following questions:

1. According to Leo, how did *Adweek* characterize the Seagram commercial?
2. On what basis does the author criticize the Bacardi Black "Taste of the night" ad campaign?
3. Why is it unlikely that beer ads will be taken off the air, in Leo's opinion?

From John Leo, "Scotch the Ads? Absolut-ly!" *U.S. News & World Report*, December 9, 1996. Copyright 1996, U.S. News & World Report. Reprinted with permission.

It could be a put-on, but *Adweek* magazine says liquor ads on television may be good for society. The magazine noted that the first booze ad shown on American TV in nearly 50 years celebrated fundamental American values. It was a Seagram commercial, placed on a station in Corpus Christi, Texas, and it featured two dogs.

One dog, labeled "obedience school graduate," carried a newspaper in its mouth. The other, carrying a bottle of Crown Royal, was labeled "valedictorian." *Adweek* said this positioned liquor as a reward for achievement and delayed gratification in a world sadly governed by instant gratification. Liquor flourished in the pre-'60s culture of self-restraint, said *Adweek*, and the impact of televised liquor ads "could well be salutary."

APPEALS TO THE YOUNG

Maybe. But it's possible to doubt that the rapid spread of self-restraint is what the distillers have in mind. The more likely long-term result is a set of psychologically clever ads aimed at young people and resulting in another upward tick or two each year in the death rate from drunk driving.

Adweek's odd commentary contains a germ of truth—one genre of liquor and beer advertising does indeed stress authority, hard work and sons following the lead of fathers. Many Scotch ads are filled with dogs, castles and other emblems of tradition, the central message being, "We know Scotch tastes like iodine, but your dad drank it and you should too." This lives on in Dewar's "Let's grow up and drink Scotch" campaign, and a Chivas Regal ad in which a grown man actually wishes his father would tell him what to do more often.

But these are upscale magazine ads aimed at the well off. Do not expect many dog and daddy ads once the booze industry gets revved up for the TV youth market and spots on *Seinfeld*. Instead we will see a lot of MTV imagery, Orwellian fantasies about sex and power, and Joe Camel-like appeals to the young.

PUSHING BUTTONS

The ad industry is very good at generating commercials that break down restraint and promote impulse. It's also important to know that the legal-drug business (tobacco and alcohol) accumulates a lot of private psychological research, the better to know which of our buttons to push. The generic stuff appears in marketing magazines, but the really potent findings, which result in all those manipulative and coded ads, aren't made public. No psychologist on the take has yet come forward to blow the whistle, à la Jeffrey Wigand. But now that the Federal Trade Commission is issuing subpoenas in connection with TV alcohol advertising, it surely should try to get the closely guarded research behind many beer and liquor ads.

The general rule of thumb is: The more dangerous the product, the more coded the ads are likely to be. Newport cigarettes' "Alive with pleasure" ads, for example, which seem much cleaned up nowadays, depended for years on coded themes of sexual hostility and violence running beneath all those merry scenes of outdoorsy couples at play. Among the egregious magazine ads for liquor, my favorite is the Bacardi Black "Taste of the night" campaign with its unmissable theme of night and liquor as liberators of the real you (and your darker side) from the bonds of civilized society. Just what we need in this troubled culture—more promotion of everyone's darker side. The booze industry as Darth Vader.

Tony Auth. Copyright 1996, Philadelphia Inquirer. Reprinted by permission of Universal Press Syndicate. All rights reserved.

In dropping their self-imposed ban on TV ads, the distillers said they wouldn't target the young. We should be dubious. The liquor executives fear they won't be able to sell their brown drinks anymore—bourbon, Scotch and brandy have not caught on among boomers or post-boomers. The trend is toward white drinks—vodka and gin—and sweet tasting or healthy-looking drinks that disguise alcoholic content. That's why Miller is testing "alcopops," a malt-based drink that looks and tastes like lemonade. Anheuser-Busch isn't far behind. Alcopops have been successfully marketed in Britain and Australia with ads featuring lovable cartoon characters—a way of conceding that the young are indeed being targeted.

ADS SHOULD BE REGULATED

The distillers' argument about beer ads has more merit. They say a can of beer has about as much alcohol as a mixed drink, so either ban beer from TV or let liquor ads on. In fact, some conspiracy theorists think the distillers' real goal is to drive beer off TV. That's extremely unlikely. Beer is so entrenched in TV economics that it's hard to imagine the sort of social upheaval necessary to drive it away. But if beer and liquor ads are going to be on TV, the ads should be regulated in the public interest. Alcohol is really a drug, and we have a long tradition of regulating drug ads to protect the public. The makers of Rogaine or Prozac aren't permitted to say whatever they wish in ads. Why should the good-tasting narcotics be exempted?

The regulation might cover TV only—our most emotional medium and the one watched most closely by children. It could curb appeals to children as well as devious psychological manipulation of adults along the lines of Bacardi's Darth Vader print ad. We know that the televising of liquor ads will promote accelerated consumption, with predictable increases in addiction and drunk driving. If we can't stop it, let's at least set some sensible rules that reflect the true social costs involved.

| "There is not a single study—not one study in the United States or internationally—that credibly connects advertising with an increase in alcohol use or abuse."

TELEVISION LIQUOR ADS WILL NOT PROMOTE UNDERAGE DRINKING

Morris E. Chafetz

Morris E. Chafetz is the president and founder of the Health Education Foundation, an organization that develops health promotion programs for government and the business community. In the following viewpoint, Chafetz contends that the public should not be alarmed by the fact that the liquor industry has ended its forty-eight-year self-imposed ban on TV liquor ads. Insisting that there is no proof that alcohol advertising causes people to drink, Chafetz disputes the contention that liquor ads on television will lead to an increase in drinking among young people. He maintains that teenagers are more likely to drink if alcohol is characterized as "forbidden fruit" than if it is promoted on television.

As you read, consider the following questions:

1. According to the author, who should decide whether manufacturers of distilled spirits should advertise on television?
2. How are members of the print media being hypocritical on the issue of alcohol advertising, in Chafetz's opinion? How does he say they rationalize their hypocrisy?
3. What attitude should society have toward young people, in the author's opinion?

From Morris E. Chafetz, "Facts About Kids, Booze, and TV," Chicago Tribune, December 23, 1996. Reprinted with permission of Knight-Ridder/Tribune Information Services.

I've been an interested observer of the debate on ending the distilled spirits industry's self-imposed 48-year moratorium on TV advertising. As a psychiatrist, scientist and former national architect of ways to reduce alcohol problems, I have always sought to marshal the best science, both biomedical and behavioral, to reduce alcohol abuse. I think the focus by advocacy groups on advertising and the availability of alcohol as the major contributor to alcohol problems misses the mark.

Critics are raising the specter that television liquor advertising will increase alcohol abuse and underage drinking. If I believed that banning these ads from TV would keep a bottle out of the hands of a child or a person with an alcohol-abuse problem, I would lead the charge against lifting the moratorium.

Instead, I find myself asking an important question: Where in the name of science is there any proof? If alcohol ads will end society as we know it, shouldn't there be some science to say it's so?

No Connection Between Ads and Behavior

I come to this issue as a psychiatrist and scientist, nothing more. It's not my business whether manufacturers of distilled spirits should or should not advertise on TV. That is—quite literally—their business, something more appropriate for an MBA than an M.D. to decide. What I can say is that opponents of TV advertising for distilled spirits (or any other alcohol beverage for that matter) assert a connection between ads and the altering of behavior that, scientifically speaking, just isn't there.

As I've written in the *New England Journal of Medicine*, there is not a single study—not one study in the United States or internationally—that credibly connects advertising with an increase in alcohol use or abuse. Any assertion or assumption that alcohol ads increase use and abuse is fantasy, not fact.

The hypocrisy concerning advertising is reflected in a recent newspaper editorial against liquor ads in the name of protecting the health of youngsters. So far as I know, no newspaper is ready to forgo liquor ads and the revenue liquor advertisements bring. Members of print media rationalize their hypocrisy by calling "television the medium most likely to reach most members of potential underage drinking." The old adage that it's easy to give advice one does not have to take operates here.

Respect Young People

Advice or not, advocacy groups continue to operate as though young people must be protected from knowing about the [dishonor] of the adult world. We take statistics about all kinds of problems and twist them into causes we can rise against. As a physician and researcher, I know this to be true.

As a father and grandfather, I've noticed through the years that young people are not Pavlovian in their responses. Billions of dollars are spent each year bombarding young people with ads for all kinds of products, some of which they covet and others which they ignore.

The public ought to stop worrying about the power of ads and focus on the power of prohibition: the unintended consequences of demonizing a product or behavior. Never underestimate the seductive power of a "Thou Shalt Not."

The natural impulse to go against the grain is a reality of adolescent life. Forbidden fruit is an old story, but it's one with enduring power. I ponder the question countless times: Are anti-drinking advocacy groups—unintentionally or not—the most effective marketers for underage drinking?

As we debate the issue of advertising distilled spirits on TV, let's do so with open eyes. We need to respect young people more than we now do. They will take their risks as we did when we were adolescents. Ignorance does not lead to abstinence.

And let's also remember that when we invoke science to dress prejudice as policy, we do more than simply distort science. We demean policy and the laws we live by as well.

> "Both the actual number and percentage of alcohol billboards are much greater in minority neighborhoods. . . . Alcohol marketers have clearly singled out minorities."

THE ALCOHOL INDUSTRY TARGETS MINORITY NEIGHBORHOODS

Diana P. Hackbarth, Barbara Silvestri, and William Cosper

Diana P. Hackbarth is a professor of community, mental health, and administrative nursing at Loyola University in Chicago. Barbara Silvestri is the director of Smoking or Health at the American Lung Association of Metropolitan Chicago (ALAMC). William Cosper is a research assistant at ALAMC. In the following viewpoint, the authors describe their study of alcohol and tobacco billboards in Chicago. They report that the number of alcohol and tobacco billboards is greater in minority neighborhoods than in white neighborhoods. According to the authors, this disparity reflects a deliberate attempt by the alcohol and tobacco industries to saturate minority neighborhoods with messages to purchase and consume dangerous products.

As you read, consider the following questions:

1. Why do the authors say they included alcohol advertising in their study?
2. Why does outdoor advertising of alcohol and tobacco raise "special public health concerns," according to the authors?
3. What is the ratio of alcohol billboards in minority neighborhoods as compared to white neighborhoods, according to the authors?

From Diana P. Hackbarth, Barbara Silvestri, and William Cosper, "Tobacco and Alcohol Billboards in Fifty Chicago Neighborhoods: Market Segmentation to Sell Dangerous Products to the Poor," Journal of Public Health Policy, vol. 16, no. 2, 1995. (Notes/references in the original have been omitted here.) Reprinted by permission.

In 1990, the American Lung Association of Metropolitan Chicago (ALAMC) joined together with other health advocacy and community groups to promote legislation to ban billboard advertising of tobacco products within the city of Chicago. The impetus for this legislation came from a variety of sources. Several community groups had observed that predominantly poor and minority neighborhoods in Chicago were inundated with billboards pushing tobacco and alcohol products. Parents and community leaders were concerned about the effect on their children of daily exposure to scores of billboards encouraging them to smoke and drink. The *Chicago Reporter*, a local newspaper which primarily serves the African-American community, featured an exposé on unlicensed billboards, political contributions, and alcohol and tobacco advertisements. The newspaper reported on a small-scale survey of billboards located on major streets in 15 Chicago community areas. Reporters found that in poor African-American and Hispanic communities, there were both greater numbers of billboards and a higher percentage which advertised tobacco and alcohol, when compared to white communities. In addition, many billboards in poverty areas were unlicensed, a violation of Chicago zoning laws.

At the same time, an activist priest was engaged in a high-profile campaign to deface billboards in his predominantly poor African-American parish as a way to call media attention to the problem. Subsequently a member of the Chicago City Council responded to community concern by holding hearings on proposed legislation to ban all outdoor advertising of tobacco products in Chicago.

However, despite intense community and media interest in the problem, no data base existed which encompassed the entire city and scientifically documented the pattern of tobacco and alcohol billboard placement. Therefore, the American Lung Association of Metropolitan Chicago initiated a study in which all billboards in Chicago were counted and the advertising themes noted. These data were then matched with information on population and race from the 1990 census in order to document which areas of the city, if any, were burdened by excess tobacco billboards. Outdoor advertising of alcohol was also included in the study, both because of the adverse effect of excess alcohol consumption on health and because alcohol and tobacco often act together as "gateway drugs" which pave the path to illicit drug use by adolescents. However, no legislation banning billboard advertising of alcoholic beverages was under consideration at the time of the study.

Cigarettes are one of the most heavily advertised products in America. The tobacco industry spends almost four billion dollars per year touting their dangerous products. Tobacco and alcohol companies rank among the top five advertisers in magazines and newspapers. The top four billboard advertisers are all tobacco companies, and cigarettes have long reigned as the most heavily advertised product in the outdoor media. In 1993, ads for beer, wine and liquor ranked seventh, while billboard advertising of tobacco fell to second place for the first time. Liquor ads account for almost 20% of transit shelter advertisements, while cigarette ads account for 15%. Outdoor advertising of tobacco and alcohol is responsible for about 1.6 billion dollars in revenues annually, or about one third of all billboard revenues nationwide. Recent trends in cigarette advertising suggest that increasing emphasis is being placed on promotional activities, such as consumer sampling, retail promotions, and sponsorships of athletic, entertainment, civic or cultural events. These promotions are often targeted at specific segments of the potential market, such as women, African-Americans, Hispanic-Americans, and children and adolescents.

A FIXTURE OF THE GHETTO

The liquor store is such a fixture of the modern ghetto that sometimes it hardly seems worth mentioning. . . . When 1992's riot erupted, South Central Los Angeles had a staggering 728 licensed liquor outlets—13 per square mile. Roughly half were convenience stores that sold beer and wine; the rest sold hard liquor as well. To put those numbers in perspective, South Central had more stores selling hard liquor than 13 entire states can claim and a liquor outlet at virtually every major intersection.

David Whitman and David Bowermaster, *U.S. News & World Report*, May 31, 1993.

Outdoor advertising of tobacco and alcohol is a form of advertising which raises special public health concerns. While no one is forced to read advertisements in magazines or watch beer commercials on television, motorists and pedestrians, including nonsmokers, nondrinkers and children, can't avoid exposure to outdoor advertising. Publications specifically aimed at minors do not routinely accept tobacco and liquor advertisements. However, the billboard industry has historically exercised little restraint on placement of its ads. In June 1989 the Outdoor Advertising Association of America responded to public criticism and adopted a voluntary code for advertising which is supposed to assure that tobacco and alcohol ads are at least 500 feet from schools, churches and hospitals. The code is also designed to set voluntary limits on the number of billboards in a market that advertise products which can't legally be sold to minors.

However, this voluntary code is often ignored. Billboards are placed for maximum visibility in designated markets in order to maximize revenues. Information on the demographic make-up of the community in which ads are placed is used to seg-ment the market. Billboard ads are created to match the demo-graphic makeup and socioeconomic characteristics of the market. Billboards advertising tobacco and alcohol can be found near mom and pop grocery stores, shopping centers, fast food restaurants, near homes and day care centers, along major streets, expressways, on mass transit lines and in sports stadi-ums, all places where young people would be likely to congre-gate. The result of this strategy is that America's children have maximum exposure to custom-designed outdoor advertising encouraging them to use potentially dangerous products which they cannot legally purchase. . . .

SATURATING POOR AND MINORITY NEIGHBORHOODS

Another issue unique to outdoor advertising is the focus of this study: market segmentation aimed at saturating poor and mi-nority neighborhoods with messages to buy and use dangerous products. Despite vociferous denials by the tobacco and alcohol industry, and the Outdoor Advertising Association of America's voluntary code, evidence suggests that saturation of poor and minority neighborhoods with tobacco and alcohol billboards is a common phenomenon. Scenic America, a nonprofit member-ship organization which advocates billboard and sign control, compiled a summary of billboard surveys conducted by various groups between 1986–1989 in several major American cities. In Baltimore, 76% of billboards in African-American neighbor-hoods advertised alcohol and tobacco, compared to 20% in white neighborhoods. In Detroit, the ratio was 56% to 38%, and in St. Louis, 62% to 36%. Community groups in New Orleans, Washington, D.C., and San Francisco reported a similar pattern. While the methods and comprehensiveness of the billboard sur-veys varied in each of the cities studied, the results all point in the same direction. Poor and minority areas of many American cities are inundated with billboards advertising tobacco and al-cohol products. . . .

African-Americans are an important market segment for both tobacco and alcohol companies. African-Americans are more likely to smoke menthol cigarettes than whites. Newport, Kool and Salem, along with Winston, are heavily marketed to this community. Eight-sheet billboards, which are small (5' x 11') and low to the ground, are abundant in minority communities in many large cities. These billboards feature African-American models who are uniformly healthy, well dressed and glamorous, smoking cigarettes or drinking malt liquor or cognac. Partying and sex appeal are major advertising themes.

Hispanics are another market segment which has been targeted by tobacco and alcohol companies. Newport, Winston, Camel and Salem are frequently advertised, along with brands aimed especially at Hispanics, such as Rio and Dorado. Eight-sheet billboards featuring Hispanic models and slogans in Spanish are common for both tobacco and liquor ads. Often emphasis is placed on encouraging Hispanic women to smoke, even though Hispanic women have traditionally not smoked as frequently as Hispanic men. Thus Hispanic women of childbearing age may be considered a "developmental market" for the tobacco companies.

THE STUDY

The study [is a] survey of all billboards located within the city of Chicago which were in place during the period of data collection. Wards within the city of Chicago were selected as the unit of geographic measurement for the study. Wards are the basic unit of city government and are the level at which patronage, jobs and contracts are awarded. . . .

The city of Chicago is divided into 50 wards, based on population. Each ward is mandated to have an approximately equal number of residents, about 55,000. Ward maps are gerrymandered by politicians, with race as the most important factor. . . .

Data collection extended over a nine-month period, from August 1990 to April 1991. Data was collected by the researchers as well as teams of volunteers recruited and trained by the American Lung Association of Metropolitan Chicago. Data collectors went in pairs; one driver and one counter and recorder. Each pair of data collectors had a detailed ward map and specially designed tally sheets. Data collectors drove systematically up and down every street within their assigned ward and counted all outdoor billboard advertisements. Billboards were defined as freestanding outdoor signs; signs attached to buildings; advertisements painted on buildings; and placards, posters and devices which are used to advertise on any public way, street or alley. Signs identifying the name of a business and advertising signs inside or on the windows of businesses were excluded. All billboards which met these criteria in the city of Chicago were included in the study. Tobacco and alcohol billboards were tallied separately from those advertising other products and services. In the case of tobacco billboards, the address of the billboard, content or advertising theme, brand of tobacco product, and location near schools, parks, day care centers or other places where children congregate were also noted. Three categories of content of outdoor advertising were noted: billboards advertising tobacco products; billboards advertising alcoholic beverages; and all "other" billboards. No attempt was made to ascertain whether or not the billboards were licensed, as this was not the focus of the study.

For ease in analysis and clarity in presentation to alderpersons and community leaders, wards in Chicago were dichotomized into two groups based on population by race in the 1990 census. Wards with less than 50% minority residents were classified as white. Wards with 50% or more minority residents were classified as minority. Using this classification, 16 wards were classified as white and 34 as minority.

Descriptive statistics were calculated. In addition, correlations between the number and percent of minority residents per ward and the number and percent of tobacco and alcohol billboards were calculated.

MINORITY NEIGHBORHOODS ARE INUNDATED

The total number of billboards identified in the study was 5924. The minimum number of billboards in any ward was 17 and the maximum was 309. The median number of billboards per ward was 113 and the mean was 118.

The total number of billboards was compared in the 16 white versus 34 minority wards. There were 805 billboards in white wards and 5119 in minority wards. Thus 86.4% of all billboards are located in minority wards, despite the fact that minority wards are home to only 66% of the population. Therefore, there are about 31% more billboards in minority wards than would be expected based on population. Stated as rates, there were 27.8 billboards per 10,000 population in minority wards compared to 8.5 per 10,000 in white wards. The mean number of billboards per ward in minority wards was 150, compared to 50 in white wards. These data verify easily observed anecdotal evidence that poorer, minority neighborhoods are inundated with many more billboards than white neighborhoods, which are generally more affluent and better able to control their environment.

Advertising themes in outdoor advertising were the main focus of the study. Tobacco billboards constituted 24.5% of all billboards in Chicago. The minimum number of tobacco billboards per ward was 3 and the maximum was 117. The median number of tobacco billboards per ward was 24 and the mean was 29. Alcohol billboards constituted 23.9% of all billboards in Chicago. Some wards had as few as one alcohol billboard while others had as many as 111. The median number of alcohol billboards per ward was 23 and the mean was 28. These data reveal that 48.4% of billboards in Chicago advertised alcohol or tobacco products.

COMPARING THE NUMBERS

The number of tobacco billboards in the 16 white and 34 minority wards was compared. In white wards, the number of tobacco billboards ranged from 3 to 25 with a mean of 13. In minority wards, the minimum number of tobacco billboards was 8 and the maximum 117. The mean number of tobacco billboards in minority wards was 36. Therefore minority wards, on average, had almost three times as many tobacco billboards as white wards.

TABLE I

Comparison of the Number of Alcohol Billboards
in White and Minority Wards*

TOTAL ALCOHOL BILLBOARDS IN WHITE WARDS = 115

    Minimum per ward = 1
    Maximum per ward = 15
    Mean per ward   = 7

TOTAL ALCOHOL BILLBOARDS IN MINORITY WARDS = 1300

    Minimum per ward = 1
    Maximum per ward = 111
    Mean per ward   = 38

Minority wards have an average of more than five times as many alcohol billboards as white wards

*White wards = 16
Minority wards = 34

A similar picture of ward saturation emerges when alcohol billboards are compared in white and minority wards. The number of alcohol billboards in white wards ranged from 1 to 15 with a mean of 7. In contrast, in minority wards, the minimum number of alcohol billboards was 1 and the maximum was 111. The mean number of alcohol billboards in minority wards was 38. These data demonstrated that, on average, minority wards are burdened with more than five times as many billboards touting alcohol as white wards (See Table I).

The combined number of alcohol and tobacco billboards were compared in white versus minority wards. In white wards, a mean of 20 billboards per ward advertise alcohol or tobacco and in minority wards a mean of 74 billboards advertise the same dangerous products. In white areas of the city, about 40% of billboards advertise alcohol or tobacco, and in minority areas, 49% of billboards advertise these products. These percentages may be compared with data from the 1990 *Chicago Reporter* study of 15 community areas which found that 49% of the billboards surveyed advertised either alcohol or tobacco.

EXPLORING CORRELATIONS

Another way to examine the data is to explore the correlation between the percent of minority residents in a ward and the number of tobacco and alcohol billboards.

These data illustrate that there is a significant positive correlation between the percent of minority residents in a ward and placement of alcohol and tobacco billboards, confirming that minority neighborhoods are more likely to have billboards hawking dangerous products than white areas of the city.

The percent of alcohol and tobacco billboards may also be compared to the percent of minority residents.

These data illustrate that both the actual number and percentage of alcohol billboards are much greater in minority neighborhoods than in white areas of the city. Alcohol marketers have clearly singled out minorities. In the case of tobacco, the number of tobacco billboards is greater in minority areas, but the percentage of billboard ads extolling the virtues of tobacco is not significantly greater than the percentage in white areas of the city. In addition, the ratio of approximately three times as many billboards advertising tobacco in minority neighborhoods corresponds to the finding of approximately three times as many billboards of all types in minority wards compared to white wards. However, the practical implications of percentages of billboards are unclear. A child walking to school in an African-American or Hispanic neighborhood is three times more likely to see a tobacco billboard than a child residing in a predominantly white neighborhood, even though the percentages of billboards advertising tobacco may be similar in white and minority wards. Thus the absolute number of advertising messages to smoke and drink, rather than the percentage of billboards carrying the message, seems to be most relevant.

"It is naive to think that crime and violence will diminish by banning adult beverage outdoor billboards."

THE ALCOHOL INDUSTRY BENEFITS MINORITY NEIGHBORHOODS

Noel N. Hankin

Noel N. Hankin is the director of corporate relations at the Miller Brewing Company. The following viewpoint is a speech he delivered to the California State Package Store and Tavern Owners Association (Cal Pac) in Los Angeles on May 13, 1994. Hankin argues that the alcohol industry is being unfairly blamed for problems in black communities. Crime and violence in minority neighborhoods are not caused by alcohol and alcohol advertising, he contends, but by a lack of educational and employment opportunities for young people. Hankin insists that the alcohol industry benefits the black community by creating jobs, generating tax revenues, and providing scholarships to local youths.

As you read, consider the following questions:

1. How did the mood in the black community change in the 1980s, according to Hankin?
2. Why did some community leaders begin to focus on the alcohol industry in the 1990s, in the author's opinion?
3. What steps does Hankin recommend for improving press coverage of the alcohol industry?

From Noel N. Hankin, "The Licensed Beverage Industry in the African-American Community: Scapegoat or Force for Economic Growth?" a speech delivered May 13, 1994, to the California State Package Store and Tavern Owners Association, Los Angeles, California.

In most parts of the world, to own an establishment that is licensed to serve beverage alcohol would be considered prestigious. In South America, Europe, Asia and even in parts of Africa, you would be looked up to in a similar manner as professional people and certainly other successful business owners.

But here in America, producers of beer and other licensed beverages, along with your retail industry, are often viewed as being the reason for a series of problems in our communities. We get blamed for virtually everything that is wrong in our society.

The reasons are complex but can be better understood by looking back over the recent past. In college my major was sociology, and in the business world I make my living in marketing. When I combine these disciplines in examining recent history, some very interesting and clear conclusions come into focus.

Recently, I reviewed a large number of the important events that occurred in each decade, starting with the 1950's, up to the present. By discarding extraneous and unrelated factors and focusing just on incidents and events that relate to our current situation, a clear story emerges: a story that says our industry is not the reason why there are such severe problems in our community.

In fact, the opposite is actually a more reasonable observation. Our industry has made *significant* contributions toward the betterment of our community.

Let's take a short walk through time to see how we got to where we are today.

THE 1950'S

• In the 50's, we fought for desegregation.
• Thurgood Marshall, the lead attorney for the NAACP, won a landmark decision that desegregated the nation's public schools.
• Emmett Louis Till was murdered for speaking to a white woman.
• Rosa Parks refused to give up her seat to a white man.
• The Little Rock Nine stood up to Governor Orval Faubus of Arkansas.
• Author Richard Wright coined the phrase "Black Power" in one of his books.
• Willie Mays took the game of baseball to a new level.
• The Interstate highway system was built, and the auto industry took off, ushering in a new era of mobility.

Our mood in the black community during the 50's (we were Negroes back then) was one of optimism. Sure we were suffering from institutionalized and de facto racism, but we *were* making progress.

New opportunities were opening up on a regular basis. Some even felt we were moving too fast—remember that? With this as a backdrop, Cal Pac was founded in 1960. Let's take a look at some of the highlights of the 60's.

THE 1960'S

• The civil rights movement was in full swing—picketers, sit-ins, freedom riders, and in California, Black Panthers.

• George Wallace said, "Segregation now. Segregation tomorrow. Segregation forever."

• Medger Evers was murdered as were [civil rights workers] Michael Schwerner, Andrew Goodman and James Chaney.

• MLK [Martin Luther King Jr.] had a dream and was assassinated; JFK [John F. Kennedy] was assassinated and so was his brother.

• In Selma, Alabama, 200 state troopers attacked and beat black marchers, using tear gas, nightsticks and whips.

• Stokely Carmichael popularized the phrase "Black Power"—he obviously read Richard Wright's book.

• Vietnam was in full rage: 50,000 Americans died—many under the age of 18.

• Virtually every fit male over the age of 18 was drafted.

• The Army became the most significant equal opportunity employer—at least at the lower ranks; after Vietnam wound down, some parents wanted their sons in the Army to give them a sense of discipline and so they could learn a trade or qualify for educational opportunities when they got out.

• Wilt Chamberlain scored 100 points.

• Fatalities on the highway increased; we learned what DWI means.

• For those who could afford a car, there was limitless mobility, which changed what used to be stable communities; this affected both white and black communities and began a slow process of resegregation, the magnitude of which would not be understood fully for the next two decades.

The 60's were characterized by a feeling that we would actually overcome; that we would chip away at racism and over time it would all be gone. The debate of the day in our communities was not "where are we going" but rather 'what is the best way to get there."

H. Rap Brown said, "Violence is as American as cherry pie," while others felt we could avoid violence by moving a little slower. Now on to the 1970's.

The 1970's

• In the 70's, our nation's economy continued to grow; income increased significantly, minimum wage shot up; but also inflation ran amok and with gasoline shortages, economy car sales took off and shifted many blue collar jobs to Japan.

• Affirmative action encouraged some of the larger employers to hire blacks—in some cases for the first time.

• Many black-owned businesses were created in the 70's: *Essence* and *Black Enterprise* magazines; Mingo Jones, Uniworld and Burrell advertising agencies; Fedco Foods in New York—Bruce Llewellyn's successful chain of supermarkets—and others.

• Supreme Court ordered busing to end segregation in public schools.

• Increased availability of automobiles continued to change housing and shopping patterns; driving to a mall became a social event and contributed to a new economic shift of resources out of what were previously stable, thriving black neighborhoods.

• Southern blacks continued to migrate in big numbers to the North as well as to California, bringing with them a sanctimonious attitude toward alcohol; some countered this extreme position by overindulging—one extreme was met with another.

• Black-owned nightclubs popped up in many cities; they were able to attract blacks from a larger area than before since many blacks had a car or access to one.

• Black, red and green began to show up as a source of pride in being African American.

• Immigrants continued to pour into the United States—mostly into California; they came from Mexico, but also from various parts of Asia and northern Africa.

• California added to its reputation for being a trendsetter.

• Spiro Agnew resigned followed by Richard Nixon while Watergate made names like John Erlichman, H.R. Haldeman, John Mitchell and John Dean synonymous with a new level of distrust in government.

• Charlie Smith, who was purported to be the nation's last living slave, died at the age of 137.

While the 70's were filled with much disillusionment, most of us remained optimistic. Some black-owned businesses were growing, the private sector began hiring and in a few instances, some of us even moved up the corporate ladder a notch or two.

Plus the military continued to provide an opportunity for skills training for many black youth. Black ad agencies helped to increase the number of positive images of us on television as black magazines and newspapers continued to tell our story our way.

THE 1980's

• As we moved into the 1980's, the suburbs continued to experience a growth boom; housing patterns revealed a consistent national pattern of re-segregation.

   • Divorce rate hit 49 percent (it's higher among blacks).

   • AIDS was diagnosed for the first time.

   • Martin Luther King Day became a legal holiday.

   • Jesse Jackson ran for president—twice—and kept hope alive.

   • Doug Wilder and David Dinkens were voted in [as governor of Virginia and mayor of New York, respectively].

   • *Oakland Tribune* became black-owned.

   • Drinking age was raised to 21, which began a long-term decline in on-premise adult beverage sales.

   • Some immigrant groups continued to make significant inroads into the packaged goods retail business—particularly in black neighborhoods.

A Defense of Specialized Advertising

Marketing products differently to different consumer segments is a time-honored tradition among businesses. In today's marketplace, it is the unenlightened business that refuses to acknowledge the rich cultural diversity that exists between men and women and between various ethnic groups. . . .

Still, there are some people who, because of their opposition to all alcohol consumption, criticize specialized advertising for specific consumer segments. In attacking this practice, these antialcohol activists mistakenly—yet purposefully—link advertising with alcohol abuse, and therefore claim that special marketing efforts must necessarily result in abuse by a particular market segment. They are wrong.

A significant body of research shows no link between advertising and alcohol abuse.

Jeffrey G. Becker, *Business and Society Review*, Fall 1992.

• The first reported billboard whitewashing occurred in Chicago.

The 80's represented a wake-up call in the black community. The desire to follow orders and do what is expected began to change.

Despite some significant political gains, there was a growing sense of unfairness and a lack of control and power. The notion that we could fit into society as accepted equals disappeared for many African Americans.

As evidenced by the fall of so many public figures, the motive for many decisions seemed to be based, all too often, on greed. The rallying cry for us changed from "Equal access" to "Economic empowerment."

THE 1990's

Now we are in the 90's—and so far during this decade, a lot has already happened that is shaping our lives.

• Integration became a tarnished goal—in a national survey 65 percent of all blacks said that integration will not come in their lifetime, if ever.

• Sixty-six percent of black schoolchildren attend predominantly segregated schools.

• Crime and violence emerged as #1 issue for many Americans.

• A trend toward targeted government control emerged in central city locations with various restrictions such as new rules for billboard advertising, restricted hours of licensed beverage sales, tighter controls of the density of licensed establishments, increases in cost of licenses, and so forth.

• There are curfews for young people and lots of new ideas about how to educate them: Afrocentric curricula, choice options, charter schools, black male academies, and other ideas.

• Military was essentially removed as an option for many blacks because at least five candidates exist for each available opening.

• Politically, there was a shift to the right, despite the election of Bill Clinton.

• Rodney King beating highlighted issue of racial stereotypes and equality; verdict-related disturbances destroyed many liquor stores, half of which were never re-opened.

• Corporate downsizing added an additional strain on blacks just from the sheer numbers of those who were pushed out.

The mood in the black community now is characterized by an unclear perception of our situation. There is a renewed focus on turning inward toward our own communities for solutions to the apparent problems.

However, there is also an understanding that many aspects of our lives cannot be easily controlled, such as crime, violence and the presence of illegal drugs. Therefore, for a few community leaders, there has been a focus on the things that they can control—even if those things are not the source of the problem.

Our industry falls into that category. It is naive to think that crime and violence will diminish by banning adult beverage outdoor billboards. In fact, if all adult beverages were totally eliminated, our community's problems would still not go away.

That's because the problems in our communities have to do with a lack of opportunity. Our youths do not believe, often for good reason, that they have a chance to be successful in this world.

They have these attitudes because society has systematically shut them out; they were burned by institutionalized racism and individual prejudices. Without major increases in educational and job opportunities, the feelings of hopelessness are not likely to go away and the crime and violence will continue to grow. As they grow, they will continue to put pressure on our industry.

THE BEVERAGE INDUSTRY CAN BENEFIT THE COMMUNITY

As we look back over the decades, the lesson learned is that we must strengthen our commitment to our communities and to each other. In other words, we must be able to count on each other.

The worst thing we could do as a people is to attack each other and further divide our interests and resources. The more unified we are—regardless of where we live, work or stand politically—the stronger we become. United we stand, divided we fall.

If I may paraphrase a statement of President Clinton, I firmly believe that there is nothing wrong in black communities that can't be corrected by what is right in black communities, and black-owned businesses such as yours are among the things that are right in our communities.

Right now we are at a critical juncture—we can go forward or backward. The decision will come from leaders, leaders like Cal Pac.

I encourage you to build on your existing record of service by taking the offensive, seizing the initiative and demonstrating leadership in your communities.

If we continue to build positive relationships, and if we focus on working together to address the root causes of problems, then we will emerge with real power, the power to continue to build on the economic strength that you have already started.

In order to build an economic base, we need to start with what we have. Our community's strongest economic force is the licensed beverage industry—your industry.

By the way, this industry is not only the #1 employer in the black community, but also in white communities as well. Your hospitality industry, which I will define as anyone licensed to sell adult beverages, employs more people and pays more taxes than any other black-owned group of businesses.

You are on a leading edge of the growing service industry. Your employees learn how to work with the public, how to serve customers, and how to resolve customer complaints. They also learn about pricing, ordering, inventory management, merchandising, display building, advertising and promotion, and how to build a positive reputation for your business. These are all transferable qualities, traits and skills that can be used throughout the service sector.

You should be proud that you are making such a significant contribution. Furthermore, the community should feel proud of you too.

You serve on important boards, you participate in public policy debates and help to effect positive decisions for our communities, and—unlike many other business people who can't wait to get out at the end of the day—you tend to live right in the neighborhood.

All of these things are true before you even begin to count the value of your good citizenship, the taxes you pay, your efforts to keep your neighborhoods clean and of course the scholarships that you provide to deserving youths in your area. We already talked about the significance of providing educational opportunities as part of what we need to turn our communities around, jobs being the other.

THE NEED FOR POSITIVE PRESS COVERAGE

I believe you deserve far more recognition for all the good things that you are already doing. If nobody knows what you are doing, it's almost the same as doing nothing.

So it's important to do whatever it takes to get more positive press coverage. I know that you are already doing a lot to increase awareness of your contributions, and I would encourage you to redouble your efforts in areas such as:

• Partnering with community newspapers and the local branch of the NAACP;

• Arranging for radio interviews to discuss your scholarship programs;

• Increasing your visibility on the local chamber of commerce, and writing letters to editors and elected officials to set the record straight on even small issues.

In conclusion I would like to quote a Swahili proverb that is very appropriate to the theme of what your businesses are all about: "There are three things which if a man does not know he cannot live long in the world: what is too much for him, what is too little for him, and what is just right for him."

No matter what the language, no matter what the age in history, and no matter what the culture, virtually all societies have had a conception of what the ancient Greeks called "the golden mean," and what we today call "moderation."

The bad news is that to whatever degree our products and services become associated with excess and irresponsible behavior, then to that degree we are open to attack, not only by neo-prohibitionists, but by many others in our society.

The good news is that the more strongly we in the alcohol beverage business—through our actions, our words and our examples of leadership—can associate our products and services with the concept of moderation and responsible behavior, the stronger our public image and our industry will become. There is nothing wrong with having a glass of beer and enjoying life's simple pleasures in moderation.

That's the high road, and that's the road our industry must follow.

At Miller Brewing Company, we have been involved for several years in a multi-million-dollar commitment to remind consumers to "Think When You Drink." This includes television, radio, outdoor and print advertising. The "Think When You Drink" logo appears on all company point-of-sale materials.

We pledge to you that we will continue to work with you to ensure the moderate, responsible consumption of our products, and we commend you for all the efforts you are making to create jobs, provide scholarships and offer hope in our communities all across America.

PERIODICAL BIBLIOGRAPHY

The following articles have been selected to supplement the diverse views presented in this chapter. Addresses are provided for periodicals not indexed in the *Readers' Guide to Periodical Literature*, the *Alternative Press Index*, the *Social Sciences Index*, or the *Index to Legal Periodicals and Books*.

Russell Baker	"Putting the Boot into Smoke," *New York Times*, August 27, 1996.
Jeffrey G. Becker	"Advertising and Abuse: No Link," *Business and Society Review*, Fall 1992. Available from Management Reports, Inc., 578 Post Rd. East, Westport, CT 06880.
CQ Researcher	"Alcohol Advertising," March 14, 1997. Available from 1414 22nd St. NW, Washington, DC 20037.
John J. DiIulio Jr.	"Broken Bottles: Alcohol, Disorder, and Crime," *Brookings Review*, Spring 1996.
Joel W. Grube and Lawrence Wallack	"Television Beer Advertising and Drinking Knowledge, Beliefs, and Intentions Among Schoolchildren," *American Journal of Public Health*, February 1994. Available from 1015 15th St. NW, Washington, DC 20005.
Issues and Controversies on File	"Tobacco and Alcohol Advertising," September 13, 1996. Available from Facts On File News Service, 11 Penn Plaza, New York, NY 10001-2006.
Jon Katz	"Out of the Bottle," *New York Times*, November 12, 1996.
Michael Krantz	"Seagram's on the Box," *Time*, June 24, 1996.
David Leonhardt	"A Little Booze for the Kiddies?" *Business Week*, September 23, 1996.
Antonia C. Novello	"Alcohol and Tobacco Advertising: Prevention Indeed Works," *Vital Speeches of the Day*, May 15, 1993.
Ron Scherer and Nicole Gaouette	"Critics Take Aim at the Effect of Hip Commercials on Kids," *Christian Science Monitor*, December 26, 1996.
Jeffrey Sipe	"State Sues over Wronged Sioux," *Insight*, January 22, 1996. Available from 3600 New York Ave. NE, Washington, DC 20002.
David Whitman and David Bowermaster	"A Potent Brew: Booze and Crime," *U.S. News & World Report*, May 31, 1993.

CHAPTER 3

How Should Alcoholism Be Treated?

CHAPTER PREFACE

Alcoholics Anonymous (AA) is a self-help organization whose members meet regularly to help one another stay sober. Members of AA also follow a twelve-step program that requires them to admit that they are powerless over alcohol, to turn their lives over to a "higher power," and to make amends for past and present wrongdoing. For decades, AA has been the primary treatment program for alcoholics. The organization claims nearly 2 million members in 141 countries, and its program serves as the blueprint for the medical profession's treatment of alcoholism and other forms of addiction.

Although the size and popularity of AA suggests that it offers a successful approach to treatment, in recent years many have criticized the AA program on a number of grounds. For instance, some people describe AA as a cult because it demands conformity to the AA philosophy and requires members to view themselves as powerless and in need of a higher power to help them stay sober. Ron Harders, a recovered alcoholic quoted by the *Chicago Tribune*, expresses a typical complaint about AA: "The spiritual, religious part of AA got to me. I'm not an unreligious person, but this was almost cult-like, like brainwashing. You're supposed to agree that you're not responsible for what you're doing, that you need a higher power to get over this thing."

Those who adhere to AA, however, maintain that admitting their powerlessness over alcohol was exactly what they needed to do in order to remain sober. Monica, a woman quoted by *Common Boundary* magazine, describes her experience of acknowledging her powerlessness: "I realized how unmanageable my life was. Everything was going down the drain, and I thought it was because I wasn't trying hard enough. . . . I had to understand that it wasn't within my power just to will myself to be better. . . . I needed a higher power." Other supporters acknowledge that AA is "cult-like" but insist that this characteristic is not a negative one. They contend that in order to remain sober, alcoholics need discipline and the close company of other alcoholics. "AA is definitely a cult, but a very good cult," according to Sean O'Hara, an addiction treatment administrator.

Dissatisfaction with AA has led to the development of several new organizations and methods for helping alcoholics or problem drinkers. Whether these programs are more effective than AA is one of the issues discussed in the following chapter.

| "The newest research tells us this is a disease of the brain."

ALCOHOLISM SHOULD BE TREATED AS A DISEASE

Terence T. Gorski

Many experts and laypersons disagree about whether alcoholism is a biological disease or merely a bad habit. In the following viewpoint, Terence T. Gorski defends the "disease model" of alcoholism. Although mild forms of alcoholism do not meet the definition of disease, he argues, many severe alcoholics are clearly suffering from a biological disease and should be treated accordingly by the treatment industry. Gorski is the founder and clinical director of the Relapse Prevention Certification School, which conducts training in the United States, Canada, and Europe.

As you read, consider the following questions:

1. According to Gorski, which subtypes of alcoholism meet the criteria for disease?
2. How did Maxwell Glatt damage the chemical dependency field, in the author's opinion?
3. What are the three categories of addiction, as described by Gorski?

From Terence T. Gorski, "Flawed Disease Definitions Have Hindered Alcoholism Treatment," *Professional Counselor*, October 1996. Reprinted by permission of the author.

To intelligently discuss the issue of whether alcoholism is a disease, you first have to define the disease. When talking about disease, people use three terms interchangeably: a disease; a disorder; and a syndrome.

Our working definition for use in this discussion involves three criteria:

• Does alcoholism constitute a clinical syndrome marked by an identifiable group of signs and symptoms?

• Is there a disorder present that is marked by structural or functional impairments related to the syndrome?

• Is there an etiology or cause of the syndrome that can be pinpointed or identified?

Let's address and answer the first question. Is alcoholism a syndrome? The answer to this is an absolutely unqualified "yes." You can distinguish alcoholism from other disorders. These signs and symptoms were originally identified before the turn of the twentieth century, and they've been studied and clarified ever since. Many researchers and leading professional organizations, including the American Medical Association and the American Psychiatric Association, recognize these signs and symptoms.

BODY OF KNOWLEDGE

The first modern-day medical researcher to study alcoholism, which at that time was termed "inebriety," was Dr. Benjamin Rush. His idea was that there was a syndrome of alcohol-related medical problems that he felt could best be described as a disease. His description of the symptoms was incomplete and quite primitive, but his inquiry started a process of medical examination of alcoholism as a disease.

Dr. Rush was acting against a moral model of alcoholism, which defined alcoholics as bad people, immoral sinners who needed to repent in order to get well. The framework of alcoholism as a disease was new and revolutionary.

This medical thinking culminated in the late '50s and early '60s with the research projects conducted at the Yale and Rutgers schools of alcohol studies. These studies resulted in a significant body of data that built a convincing argument that alcoholism was a disease. This body of knowledge was so compelling that the Congress of the United States created the National Institute on Alcohol Abuse and Alcoholism to nationally implement treatment programs based essentially upon this model. This work was summarized in the book, *The Disease Concept of Alcoholism*, by E.M. Jellinek, which was published in 1960.

The problem that I had all along in the field of addiction is that most people treating alcoholics never went back to this original source document, which very clearly presented an understanding of alcoholism and divided it into five subtypes:

• *Alpha* alcoholics are purely psychologically dependent but do not have physical dependence or damage. Jellinek was clear to assert that psychological dependency on alcohol alone did not constitute a disease state. Not all people with alcohol problems have the disease of alcoholism; some of them are alcohol abusers or problem drinkers who do not have the disease state.

• *Beta* alcoholics are socially and culturally heavy drinkers who were not physically addicted to the drug but suffered alcohol-related physical health problems, such as liver damage, in the absence of any pronounced signs of physical or psychological dependency. Beta alcoholism, Jellinek pointed out, is not of and by itself a disease, although the secondary damage to the organ system may be a disease.

A BIOLOGICAL DISORDER

Alcoholism is not a matter of weak will power or even a response to neurosis or other underlying psychiatric illness. What we tend to refer to as alcoholism, in the singular, should instead be referred to as "the alcoholisms" in the plural. The alcoholisms are a type of biological (biochemical) disorder in the same sense that diabetes is a biochemical disorder—although a somewhat different type to be sure. What we call diabetes is a collection of symptoms (both physical and psychological), physical signs, and laboratory studies that form a pattern that we call diabetes. . . .

We see much the same situation in "the alcoholisms." In each case we have a collection of symptoms (drinking patterns, craving, etc.), physical findings, and laboratory studies that form a pattern that we call "alcoholism."

James W. Smith, in *Alcohol Use and Misuse by Young Adults*, edited by George S. Howard and Peter E. Nathan.

• *Gamma* alcoholics exhibit progressive symptoms of both physical and psychological dependency upon alcohol. Looking retrospectively at chronic-stage alcoholism, this condition does progress and this research looked at retrospective studies only. Jellinek did view gamma alcoholism as a disease. In its end stages there was related organ-system damage, and he proposed an unknown "X factor" in terms of some function in the metabolism of the brain that created this disease state.

• *Delta* alcoholism characterizes someone physically and psychologically dependent on alcohol, but the intensity of their drinking does not increase—they drink the same amount every day. They are maintenance drinkers. Essentially, I think Jellinek was describing well controlled gamma alcoholism. He also considered delta alcoholism a disease.

• The *epsilon* alcoholic he described as the periodic alcoholic, who today we would call relapse-prone. This person has a period of sobriety, then relapses, has a binge, goes back into recovery, stays sober for a long time, then has another binge. This is a gamma alcoholic who has moved into incomplete or partial recovery and has become relapse-prone.

Gamma, delta and epsilon alcoholics represent the disease state. It's important to stress that, according to Jellinek's topology, only gamma alcoholism and its two related subtypes, delta and epsilon—the plateau drinker and the periodic binger—met the criteria for disease. The person who experienced physical consequences because of alcohol but with the absence of dependency did not, nor did the purely psychologically dependent drinker.

DAMAGE DONE

Where did we lose Jellinek's topology? Where did the damage occur?

The damage occurred because of an extremely brilliant gentleman named Dr. Maxwell Glatt. Shortly after the publication of Jellinek's disease concept, Dr. Glatt was so taken with the description of gamma alcoholism that he took the symptoms, operationalized them and put them on a chart, which he dubbed the Jellinek Chart. Try and find the Jellinek Chart in any of Jellinek's published works. You won't, because Maxwell Glatt published it in the *British Journal of Addictions*.

He then proposed a course of recovery. What Dr. Glatt did was operationalize gamma alcoholism so well that everyone became hypnotized by it. Here was a fundamental error inadvertently interjected into the consciousness of the chemical dependency field: that there is only one type of alcoholism, gamma alcoholism; that it is chronic, progressive, and eventually fatal; that everyone who has any kind of alcohol problem has the disease; and that if you have mild or early-stage alcoholism, the progression is inevitable.

This is a fundamental error that flawed the chemical dependency field and led to neglecting and failing to respond to the needs of non-addicted abusers and non-addicted problem drinkers. When these people came to us for help, we took two inexcusable positions that said, "Take treatment you don't need" or "Keep drinking until you get really sick, then come back." Both of these positions were stock and trade in many chemical dependency programs.

Dr. Glatt later published an extensive book on alcoholism that presented his full overview, but unfortunately that book never became as popular as his simple, easy-to-use Jellinek Chart.

Simultaneously, a gentleman named Mark Keller, operating under the auspices of the World Health Organization, put together a cross-cultural, international lexicon of terms involving diagnostic labels for alcoholism, basically confirming that the phenomenon of alcoholism—this thing called gamma alcoholism and the other type, the non-addicted abuser—is, in fact, a cross-cultural phenomenon.

A Biased Document

Enter the Institute of Medicine, which was commissioned to give a report to Congress. When I read that particular document, I was rather shocked because I viewed it to be a biased document primarily developed by a committee that did not understand the work that was going on in disease-model programs; did not understand the evolution of where the leading-edge thinkers were going in this field; and who really diminished the importance, at that time, of the major treatment approach to alcoholism, namely Minnesota-model treatment and its emerging and developing forms. Evidence of this is the extremely limited number of pages devoted to explaining, understanding or referencing that model, while very small, obscure behavioral studies were given pages of credit and reference.

I was really concerned when I read this because I realized that if this document went unchallenged, it would become the blueprint for reshaping chemical dependency treatment in the nation. I expressed my concerns to the leaders in the alcohol and drug treatment industry. They put together a very weak, disorganized response and let it die; that became one of the most powerful, organizing public policy documents ever published.

What we are seeing today is that the blueprint for the Institute of Medicine report is the game plan that is reorganizing service delivery for alcoholism and other drug dependency. Unfortunately, I believe it's a biased and flawed approach. It's partially correct, but it does not represent a higher-order model because biases were built in against very effective forms of treatment for very sick people. It's had, in my mind, some very dire consequences in terms of making treatment to certain subpopulations of alcoholics far less available than it was.

I think there is a broader base of treatment, but I also think there are people suffering from the disease of alcoholism who are not getting what they need publicly and privately. The document has backfired in many different ways.

DRAWING THE LINE

Let's look at it from a linear standpoint, where on one side is the non-addicted, infrequent abuser and on the other side of the line is the chronic, severely ill alcoholic. I don't know anyone who operates within a disease model of addiction who would contend that extremely mild forms of alcohol problems are a disease. They might say there are some factors that would indicate high risk, but the hardest-core disease advocate would never take a kid who got drunk for the first time and say, "You have a chronic, progressive, eventually fatal disease," and advise him to go into a long-term treatment program and never drink again.

At the other end of the line, there are some people with some very severe forms of alcoholism for whom not even the most hard-core behaviorists would say, "Gee, you don't have a disease. Your liver's falling out, you've got brain damage, you've got organ damage, you've been drinking a fifth a day for the last 12 years, you are nearly dead and in an intensive-care unit. Let's set up our little experimental drinking bar in your room and teach you how to drink in a controlled manner."

My point is, in the extreme positions there is a lot of concurrence. . . .

Where we've got the problem is the middle group. The key question is, where do we draw the line?

My basic principle is, I never knew anyone who died from abstinence. So, if in doubt, I say let's try abstinence. People with other biases say, "Well, controlled drinking is fine. If in doubt, put them on a control regimen. If it doesn't work, move toward abstinence."

The error I'd like to avoid in this discussion is what I call the "biased overgeneralization." As a disease-model advocate, I've had a lot of trouble with my colleagues who say, "Here are these people who definitely have a disease. Therefore, anyone with a drinking problem has a progressive, eventually fatal disease and should recover the way God intended him to recover, the way I did." That position is professionally untenable in my mind.

On the other hand, I have a hard time tolerating people who say, "Here's this group of patients who have alcohol problems who definitely don't meet a disease profile; therefore, nobody does and we should throw out the disease model."

A Higher Frame of Reference

What I would like to see is a higher frame of reference capable of embodying and embracing both of these points of view. I am not going to argue that people with mild alcohol and drug problems have a disease. You can't win that argument because many of them probably don't at that point. But there is definitely a group of people who do. We must protect adequate services for this population. The key question is, how do we improve our diagnostic sophistication so that we can, in fact, get better at what we do?

When you look at the disease-model research you begin to find that the major subtypes of addiction are falling into three categories:

• *Primary alcoholism*: where alcoholism develops before any other psychiatric pathology. It has two subtypes; early onset, with people who seem to be more genetically and prenatally involved; and later onset, with people who are more environmentally influenced.

• *Secondary alcoholism*: where a psychopathology, primarily antisocial disorder or conduct disorders, precede the development of addiction. There are two subsets of this; abuse disorders, and dependence disorders secondary to the psychopathology.

• *Reactive alcohol and drug abuse*: where a person drinks alcoholically and addictively in response to environmental stressors, such as Vietnam. When the person returns, the stressor is gone and they spontaneously stop or moderate their drinking.

When we're looking at the primary addiction, the newest research tells us this is a disease of the brain—specifically, a disease of brain-reward mechanisms. A person is born with a deficiency in brain-reward mechanisms, which creates a low-grade, agitated depression. When they find their drug of choice, their brain reacts by over-producing brain-reward chemicals, which produce a euphoria.

This feels so good that the person starts thinking about it a lot and develops an obsession with it. They feel an urge to do it, which is a compulsion, and this results in a craving. They have an innate, high tolerance. They're hangover-resistant, so they don't get very sick the next day.

During the '80s, the disease model brought more people into sobriety and recovery than any other approach to alcoholism or addiction treatment. The disease model does not mediate against recovery. One-third of the treatment programs were producing one-year recovery rates as high as 65 percent. They were effective.

| "Alcohol abuse can and often does lead to real, physical diseases—but it is not, in and of itself, a disease like diabetes or malaria."

ALCOHOLISM SHOULD NOT BE TREATED AS A DISEASE

Audrey Kishline

Audrey Kishline is the founder and president of Moderation Management Network, a support group network devoted to helping people reduce their drinking. In the following viewpoint, which is excerpted from her book *Moderate Drinking: The Moderation Management Guide for People Who Want to Reduce Their Drinking*, Kishline challenges the disease model of alcoholism. She points out that many experts in the field of chemical dependency reject the theory that alcoholism is a disease that can only be overcome by abstinence. Rather than requiring all problem drinkers to abstain from alcohol, Kishline asserts, treatment professionals should acknowledge that some drinking problems are less severe than others and that moderate drinking is an acceptable treatment goal for some individuals.

As you read, consider the following questions:

1. What are the three main tenets of the disease model of alcoholism, according to Kishline?
2. According to Nick Heather and Ian Robertson, quoted by the author, what has been "one of the main lines of evidence responsible for undermining disease conceptions of alcoholism"?
3. In the author's opinion, what environmental factors influence levels of alcohol use?

W hen I first had the idea of starting a moderation-oriented support group for problem drinkers, my belief that it was a workable concept and that there was a need for this type of mutual help group was little more than a hunch. I had to do some research to see if my hunch was right. It did not take me long to realize that I would need some help to accomplish this task, so I began to write to the authors of the professional literature that I was reading and I asked them for their assistance. I will never forget the flurry of journal articles that began to arrive in the mail and the number of calls and letters that I received in support of my early efforts. Over the next year, with some gentle guidance, I learned more about theories of causation, patterns of abuse, and treatment approaches for problem drinkers than I care to remember. I had to learn many Ph.D.-type words like multivariate, biopsychosocial, and psychometric, but eventually I understood the main points of the studies I read. . . .

A QUESTIONABLE THEORY

The first major revelation that I came across was that many experts in the alcohol studies field *do not believe that alcohol abuse is a disease.* From my previous experience with traditional treatment, I had been under the impression that the disease model of alcohol abuse represented a biological and medical fact, proven beyond a shadow of a doubt. I was amazed to find out that the disease theory was just that: a *theory*—one that has been highly criticized, and discarded, by many researchers in the field.

(Before going on, I should note that throughout most of this viewpoint I have put the words "alcoholic" and "alcoholism" in quotes to stress that these terms refer to a condition that *does not exist* in the sense of a biological disease, even though most non-professionals have been led to believe that they do refer to some well-defined disease. Naturally this is not meant to imply that people with alcohol abuse problems do not exist or need help.)

For example, the noted scholar Dr. Herbert Fingarette writes in his book, *Heavy Drinking: The Myth of Alcoholism as a Disease,* that "almost everything that the American public believes to be the scientific truth about alcoholism is false." Dr. Stanton Peele, author of *The Truth About Addiction and Recovery* and a leading expert in the addictions field, agrees: "Every major tenet of the 'disease' view of addiction is refuted both by scientific research and by everyday observation. This is true even for alcoholism." In 1979 the World Health Organization replaced the word alcoholism as a diagnosis with the concept of the alcohol dependence syndrome in the *International Classification of Diseases* (ICD-9). In the *Diagnostic and Statistical Manual of Mental Disorders* (DSM-IV), the American Psychiatric Association has also completely dropped a previous diagnostic class of "alcoholism" and replaced it with the disorders of alcohol abuse and alcohol dependence. Even Bill Wilson, co-founder of Alcoholics Anonymous, said the following at a convention of the National Clergy Conference on Alcoholism in 1960: "We have never called alcoholism a disease because, technically speaking, it is not a disease entity." And last, according to alcohol researchers Dr. Roger Vogler and Dr. Wayne Bartz: "Contrary to what you have been told, the excessive use of alcohol is *not* a 'disease.'"

ALCOHOL ABUSE IS A HABIT

Well, if alcohol abuse isn't a disease, what is it? In layman's terms, it is a *habit*, a learned behavior that is frequently repeated. In psychological terms it is a pattern of excessive alcohol consumption which produces maladaptive behavioral changes in which drinking can become the central activity in an individual's life, usually after many years of heavy alcohol consumption. A well-known researcher in this field, Dr. Martha Sanchez-Craig, says simply that problem drinkers "have *learned* a harmful habit." Vogler and Bartz also say that "drinking itself, including heavy drinking, is not caused by disease but by learning. You must *voluntarily* consume alcohol in fairly large amounts before you have an alcohol problem."

For the heavy drinker, this repeated behavior can eventually result in tragic consequences. Alcohol abuse can and often does *lead* to real, physical diseases—but it is not, in and of itself, a disease like diabetes or malaria. Dr. Jeffrey Schaler, an authority in the field, clearly explains this difference: "Smoking cigarettes and drinking alcohol are behaviors that can lead to the diseases we call cancer of the lungs and cirrhosis of the liver. Smoking and drinking are behaviors. Cancer and cirrhosis are diseases. Smoking and drinking are not cancer and cirrhosis."

At this point you may be saying to yourself that this whole debate about whether alcohol abuse is a disease or a behavior is just a matter of semantics, and in a way you are right. For the *chronic* drinker who is in poor health, has liver damage, and has lost his family, job, and home (that is, basically everything), the outcome of this debate really does not make a bit of difference. This is because the best solution for the severely dependent drinker is going to be the same either way: to stop drinking, completely and permanently.

For the problem drinker, however, the disease/habit debate is extremely important because it directly affects the entire approach to treating people who are beginning to have alcohol-related problems. The "learned behavior" model of drinking too much allows for what is called treatment matching. The disease model does not. Treatment matching means that the level of treatment is matched to the level of assessed problems. This is common practice in most areas of medicine.

For example, if you went to a doctor complaining of an earache, you wouldn't automatically be thrown into the hospital and hooked up to intravenous antibiotics. To start with, you would probably receive less intensive medical help for your ear infection, say a self-administered course of antibiotics. Then, if that did not work, more aggressive measures would be tried. In alcohol treatment facilities today, however, it does not matter whether you are a college student who has experienced a few binge-drinking episodes at parties or a stereotypical gutter drunk, you will both be prescribed the same "strength" of "medicine": total abstinence and, in most cases, forced or strongly suggested AA attendance.

The behavioral model of alcohol abuse allows for *less intensive*, limited intervention approaches for people who have *less severe* problems with alcohol. Moderate drinking is a permissible, and accepted, treatment goal of professional programs that offer this alternative to problem (rather than severely dependent) drinkers. Moderation itself is considered an important self-management tool for clients to acquire. In traditional treatment circles, however, the "M" word is rarely even spoken aloud.

REFUTING THE TENETS OF THE DISEASE MODEL

Why has the option of moderation for problem drinkers been such a red flag in this field for so long? It is because *all three of the main tenets of the classic disease model of alcohol abuse preclude a return to modera*-tion: irreversible progression, total loss of control, and genetic transmission. In the next few paragraphs I will quote from authorities in the addictions field who refute each of these premises, without which the disease model falls apart. (Also, and very importantly, refutation of the disease model opens the door to alternative approaches for those with less severe drinking problems.)

Let's start with irreversible progression: The disease model stipulates that once a person has problems with alcohol, those problems will inevitably get worse and worse until the untreated "alcoholic" ends up in jail, a hospital, a psychiatric ward, or the grave (whichever comes first). The problem with this belief is that it simply is not true. According to Stanton Peele, most people who go through a period of drinking problems in their lives "simply curtail or eliminate their problem drinking with age." This process is known as "maturing out," and it "occurs at all stages of the life cycle, up to and including old age." Usually, as people grow up and accept job and family responsibilities, the excessive use of alcohol becomes incompatible with their life-styles and they moderate or quit drinking on their own. From a common-sense point of view, it is obvious that if everyone who drank too much in college ended up becoming severely dependent, an incredible percentage of the population would be in treatment centers today.

In addition, the sheer number of studies that report a return to moderate drinking by former "alcoholics" has caused many experts to give up on the doctrine of irreversibility. In a comprehensive review of this subject, British researchers Dr. Nick Heather and Dr. Ian Robertson conclude: "One of the main lines of evidence responsible for undermining disease conceptions of alcoholism is the repeated finding that individuals who have been diagnosed as suffering from this disease have been able to return to drinking in a normal, controlled fashion." This is a significant finding since much of the data they reviewed was from follow-up studies of clients who went through *abstinence*-based treatment. This "disease" can hardly be called irreversible when the evidence shows that many individuals who have it return to a "non-diseased" state (moderate drinking levels). In fact, in *very* long-term follow-up studies, spanning more than 15 years, the number of abstainers and the number of those who return to moderate drinking are about equal! . . .

MISINTERPRETED RESEARCH

How did the idea of inevitable progression, which is so central to the disease concept, become popularized in the first place? In large part, it was due to the wide attention received by two journal articles written by Dr. E.M. Jellinek in 1946 and 1952, and his book, *The Disease Concept of Alcoholism*, published in 1960. This book eventually became the reference text for the disease model. Unfortunately, Jellinek's vivid descriptions of the progressively deteriorating "phases of alcohol addiction" were frequently quoted out of context by the media and by subsequent researchers. The fact that Jellinek himself cautioned that his conclusions were only tentative was largely ignored.

Jellinek's original work was based on an analysis of a questionnaire that was designed, not by Jellinek, but by Alcoholics Anonymous. Jellinek stated that he began the 1946 study "with many misgivings" because of "the small number of completed questionnaires"—there were only 98—and concerns about "the possible selectiveness of the sample"—only 6% of the questionnaires that were mailed to AA members could be used. Most importantly, Jellinek concluded that "interpretation of the data must be limited, therefore, to alcoholics of the same types as those which populate Alcoholics Anonymous groups." Again, this caution was not heeded. In Jellinek's own words:

> The lay public use the term "alcoholism" as a designation for any form of excessive drinking instead of as a label for a limited and well-defined area of excessive drinking behaviors. Automatically, the disease conception of alcoholism becomes extended to all excessive drinking irrespective of whether or not there is any physical or psychological pathology involved in the drinking behavior.

> Such an unwarranted extension of the disease conception can only be harmful, because sooner or later the misapplication will reflect on the legitimate use too and, more importantly, will tend to weaken the ethical basis of social sanctions against drunkenness.

It is crucial to realize that, after the fact, almost everything seems irreversible, and retrospective studies tend to reinforce this conceptual error. The AA survey asked respondents to list symptoms of their drinking behavior and the dates on which they first occurred. Since all the respondents were already chronic drinkers, it is not surprising that they reported a history of gradually increasing problems with alcohol. If you were to ask an overweight person if they used to weigh less, and if they gradually gained weight over time, they would also most likely answer "yes." This does not lead us to conclude, however, that the weight gain was inevitable. Many people are not aware that prospective (that is, longitudinal) studies of problem drinkers do not substantiate the claim of irreversibility.

CONTROL IS NOT LOST

What about the second premise of the disease model, that chronic drinkers are supposed to experience total loss of control if they consume even one drink that contains alcohol? "Loss of control," which many consider to be the essence of the disease model, means that once "alcoholics" start to drink, a physiological chain reaction is set in motion which makes it impossible for them to control how much they will consume and, as long as alcohol is still available, that they will invariably drink to oblivion. Many controlled laboratory studies since the 1960s have shown that when given access to alcohol, even severely dependent individuals are able to maintain considerable control over the amounts, times, and lengths of drinking sessions. These experiments, which manipulated various rewards (money, social privileges) and deprivations (no TV, isolation), demonstrated that alcohol consumption was more a matter of outside *environmental* factors than of any *internal* conditions (since the theoretical chain reaction could be put on hold, at least temporarily, and at will).

A RISK BEHAVIOR

Drinking is a risk behavior, not a disease. Both drinking and smoking can become addictive behaviors and leading causes of potentially fatal diseases like cirrhosis and cancer. The behavior is one thing, the disease consequence is another.

G. Alan Marlatt, *Professional Counselor*, October 1996.

In light of this evidence, supporters of the disease model have had to water down the "total loss of control" hypothesis. Now it is often referred to as "impaired control" or even as "variably and intermittently impaired control." These descriptions get a little closer to the truth—the ability to control alcohol consumption is not lost; it just isn't exercised. (I personally know of some people who suffer from impaired control when eating potato chips.) When people become chronic drinkers it *appears* that they have lost all control because their activities have become extremely limited, centering around two things: alcohol acquisition and consumption. But there is no scientific evidence to suggest that they have actually lost neurological control of their arm, hand, and swallowing muscles. Herbert Fingarette sums it up as follows: "The consensus among researchers today is to reject the classic idea of an alcohol-induced inability to control drinking." (Please note that this rejection of the loss of control theory does not in any way imply that people with alcohol-related problems do not need or deserve professional counseling or medical treatment for conditions caused by excessive drinking.)

AN UNSUBSTANTIATED HYPOTHESIS

Finally, what about the much-heralded genetic component of the disease concept, which proposes that "alcoholic" individuals are somehow different before they are even born? Again, this hypothesis has not been substantiated as a primary cause of excessive drinking, nor has the mysterious gene, or combination of genes, ever been located. Certain behaviors do tend to "run in families," but this does not prove a genetic link—poor manners can run in families too. It is likely that hereditary factors can increase one's susceptibility to developing alcohol problems, but many of the "susceptible" don't become "alcoholics," and some of the unsusceptible do. As Jeffrey Schaler points out, "it seems more than reasonable to attribute this variance to psychological factors such as will, volition and choice, as well as to environmental variables."

Some of the environmental factors that influence levels of alcohol use include family upbringing, peer group, job status, and marital stability. From a larger perspective, your culture and social class also have an effect on your drinking habits. Even the well-known genetic researcher Dr. Robert Cloninger stresses the importance of "variables that are critical at the population level, such as education and commercial advertising which influence exposure to alcohol by changing social attitudes and expectations about alcohol use." For example, after a long period of alcohol rationing was abolished in Sweden in 1955, there was an increase in reported alcohol-related problems among teenagers. According to Cloninger, this was most likely due to the sudden change in availability of alcohol and "attitudes toward its use for recreation, relaxation, and enjoyment," and not due to a sudden "change in the gene pool.". . .

The nature-versus-nurture debate is far from over, but most would agree that it takes a combination of both to produce human behavior. It would be fatalistic and it certainly would obviate the need for the helping professions if we were to conclude that all negative behaviors are genetically predetermined, leaving individuals incapable of change. . . .

It does not make sense to take every conceivable bad habit, tack on an "ism," and call it a disease. If a person watches too much TV, to the point of losing sleep and getting to work late, we wouldn't say that she or he is suffering from the incurable disease of "TVism." Likewise, the act of lifting a drink to your lips too often is not a "disease," using the common-sense meaning of the word. It is not transmitted from person to person by any known bacterium or virus. And, unlike real diseases, it does not take up residence at any known physical site, or in any of the systems in the human body. Drinking too much is a behavior, something that a problem drinker *does*, not something that he or she *has*.

| "What has made A.A.'s spirituality so effective in the lives of many people is . . . the specific nature of its suggestions."

ALCOHOLICS ANONYMOUS IS EFFECTIVE

Neil J. Carr

Alcoholics Anonymous (AA) is a twelve-step program for people who want to stop drinking. The twelve steps lead members through the process of admitting their powerlessness over alcohol, turning their lives over to God, confessing their wrongdoings, making amends to people they have harmed, and helping other alcoholics become sober. In the following viewpoint, Neil J. Carr praises AA as a deeply spiritual program that has helped liberate large numbers of people from addiction to alcohol. Carr, a Jesuit priest, is an associate staff member at the Jesuit Center for Spiritual Growth in Wernersville, Pennsylvania.

As you read, consider the following questions:

1. What does the asceticism of AA consist of, as Carr describes it?
2. What consolation do recovering alcoholics enjoy, according to the author?
3. Why would Augustine be appropriate as the "patron saint" of twelve-step spirituality, in Carr's opinion?

From Neil J. Carr, "Liberation Spirituality: Sixty Years of A.A." *America*, June 17, 1995. Reprinted by permission of the author.

The shout, "That's A.A.!" was one I hardly expected to hear in a graduate class of theology. But I heard it in 1994 at the Jesuit School of Theology in Berkeley, California. It was provoked by the professor's lively overview of St. Paul's Letter to the Romans. The 12 steps of Alcoholics Anonymous mirror in a remarkable way this letter of Paul. Those steps neatly package for our contemporary world not only the wisdom of Paul, but also the wisdom of the centuries, as captured in writings that go back even to pre-Christian times.

At the end of June 1995, people converged to San Diego by the thousands to celebrate their liberation from the effects of a fatal disease. To the casual observer they appeared no different from the usual conventioneers. But they weren't drinking. They were grateful members of Alcoholics Anonymous, there to mark A.A.'s 60th birthday, 60 years of rescuing over two million people around the world from the jaws of death, themselves included.

The deep spirituality of A.A.'s program of 12 steps has only recently been discovered by mainstream religious savants, who laud it now in such terms as "America's unique contribution to the history of spirituality" (Richard Rohr), and as "the greatest spiritual movement of the 20th century" (Keith Miller). I believe these claims are true.

A.A.'S 12 STEPS

What has made A.A.'s spirituality so effective in the lives of many people is, I believe, the specific nature of its suggestions. They embody ancient spiritual insights of many religions of both East and West and deliver them to people of the 20th century whose lives are unmanageable and who feel powerless to change them by their own devices. Such persons are trapped in various types of addictive behaviors. A.A.'s 12 steps have proved effective for compulsions other than drinking—gambling, narcotics, sex, eating and smoking, to name but a few.

For alcoholics, the A.A. program of 12 steps becomes a way of life. They see sobriety not as a destination, but as a journey. The alcoholic in A.A. suffers from what he or she knows is a fatal disease, presently in remission, but able to flare up at any unguarded moment. As the Big Book (*Alcoholics Anonymous*, A.A.'s "Bible," first published in 1939) explains, alcoholism is "cunning, baffling, powerful," and for that reason eternal vigilance is required. The pilgrims making the A.A. journey in sobriety can enjoy no rest stops along the way, nor can they ever escape a constantly recurring roadside warning that reads "Under Construction." The roadbed must be maintained in good repair, a task accomplished only when the alcoholic is willing to go to any length to win and persevere in sobriety. As the Big Book says, there is no "easier, softer way." The founders of A.A. learned from experience that "half measures availed us nothing."

A.A.'s third tradition states that "the only requirement for membership is a desire to stop drinking." True enough: That admits a person to the fellowship of A.A. But unless that desire is an honest one, it will never anchor him there. He must eventually fully embrace his powerlessness over alcohol in the very depth of his being.

DISCIPLINE

One of the great blessings of A.A.'s spirituality is its asceticism, the disciplinary course of conduct needed to maintain the alcoholic's prized sobriety. The A.A. member considers sobriety a precious gift, which, like all things precious, is fragile even after many years of testing and needs protection against destruction. Some treasures are subject to slow corrosion—but not sobriety. Once corrosion begins (as it does, for example, when an alcoholic begins to think he's cured and stops going to meetings), a single drink is all that is needed to begin a precipitous slide into the darkness of addiction and the misery from which he or she had once gratefully escaped. Alcoholics deeply believe that no power of their own, indeed no human aid whatever, had gained their sobriety originally and that, in the event of a fall, they can redeem themselves only with the help of a higher power, the grace of God.

To spell out the asceticism of A.A.'s way of life in great detail would be a lengthy task. In broad terms, it consists simply of regular attendance at meetings—"90 meetings in 90 days" to begin with, based on an admission of powerlessness over alcohol and hence the need for a higher power to remove the deadly obsession that had driven the alcoholic to the brink of despair. In addition, the A.A. program requires daily meditation and prayer, the reading of A.A. literature, especially the Big Book, and the application of the 12-step principles to everyday affairs. The result is an eventual spiritual awakening and the joyous life of interior freedom.

I believe it was Robert Frost who once wrote that "the best way out is through." The alcoholic finds his way out of bondage to alcohol through A.A.'s miracle of recovery. Bill Wilson, co-founder of A.A. with Dr. Bob Smith in 1935, used the word "recovery" often in composing the Big Book. The wise member of A.A., however, thinks of him or herself as recovering, lest complacency take root. Complacency would wean him from his spiritual base and allow his disease to return with even greater force than it had when he first stopped drinking. For, strangely enough, the disease progresses even during years of abstinence from alcohol, though its power to kill is arrested as long as one is not drinking.

The consolation of recovering alcoholics lies in their belief that they are exactly where God wants them to be, that somehow all the dreadful experiences of active alcoholism had a purpose. These have brought them to the happiness they now enjoy, to a freedom that they now know lay on the other side of A.A.'s discipline. For without that discipline, their way of life would lack structure.

A Spiritual Program

Bill Wilson wrote in one of his letters, "We must find some spiritual basis for living, else we die." Though not active in any particular church, he was deeply influenced by religious thought that came to him through early association with the Oxford Movement [a morality movement that originated in the 1920s] and through supporters like the Rev. Sam Shoemaker, an Episcopalian, and a Jesuit, Father Edward Dowling, whom Wilson eulogized as a close friend and who was one of his sponsors. Father Dowling was the "human being" with whom he took his all-important fifth step: "(We) admitted to ourselves, to God and to another human being, the exact nature of our wrongs."

So as not to turn away suffering alcoholics who might be agnostics or atheists, A.A. suggests to such persons that they use as their "higher power" a group of the fellowship itself whose meetings they attend regularly, and to others that they use God as they understand God. A.A. thus wisely treats the creed and worship of organized religion as not essential to the healing process, while yet encouraging church or synagogue attendance as helpful. A.A. insists that its program is spiritual, not religious, since no specific understanding of God is prescribed, but only the need for a higher power of individual choice. There is, therefore, no religious creed or liturgy connected with its meetings, although most conclude with the recitation of the Lord's Prayer. For the God mentioned in the steps is clearly personal, all-powerful and loving: the Judeo-Christian God, not a vague source of strength. The power "greater than ourselves" mentioned in the second step is a stepping stone to trust in a God who knows, loves, and is ready to help his children.

Belief in a higher power is essential to an alcoholic's journey to sobriety. "No human power," says A.A., "could have relieved our alcoholism." Yet faith is not sufficient of itself. Trust is the capstone, trust in God and in the program. In the third of the 12 steps, it is suggested that alcoholics turn their will and their lives over to the care of God as they understand him. This implies, as just mentioned, belief in a personal, loving God in whom they must put their trust.

THE TWELVE STEPS OF ALCOHOLICS ANONYMOUS

1. We admitted we were powerless over alcohol—that our lives had become unmanageable.

2. Came to believe that a Power greater than ourselves could restore us to sanity.

3. Made a decision to turn our will and our lives over to the care of God *as we understood Him.*

4. Made a searching and fearless moral inventory of ourselves.

5. Admitted to God, to ourselves, and to another human being the exact nature of our wrongs.

6. Were entirely ready to have God remove all these defects of character.

7. Humbly asked Him to remove our shortcomings.

8. Made a list of all persons we had harmed, and became willing to make amends to them all.

9. Made direct amends to such people wherever possible, except when to do so would injure them or others.

10. Continued to take personal inventory and when we were wrong promptly admitted it.

11. Sought through prayer and meditation to improve our conscious contact with God *as we understood Him,* praying only for knowledge of His will for us and the power to carry that out.

12. Having had a spiritual awakening as the result of these steps, we tried to carry this message to alcoholics, and to practice these principles in all our affairs.

Alcoholics Anonymous (the "Big Book"), 3rd edition, 1976.

The spectator at a circus who peers up at a man on the high wire pushing a wheelbarrow across from one end to the other feels very certain that the performer will arrive at the other end without incident. But if he had trust, he would be willing somehow to climb up there and sit in the wheelbarrow. That is quite a difference, yet that is the kind of trust in God and the program asked of the alcoholic. Once in the wheelbarrow, however, the alcoholic becomes part of the act, a very essential part, and is greatly responsible for preserving the balance. This is where a rigorous fidelity to living the 12 steps becomes all-important. Such personality flaws as projection or retrospection—leaning in one direction or the other—can disturb the balance and court disaster. Consequently, these and other character defects, such as surrendering to impulses toward pride, anger and other primordial instincts, must be curbed, a life-long process of both purification and enrichment.

COMPLETE SURRENDER

A.A.'s spiritual liberation has deep roots in the religious traditions of the ages, going beyond the Judeo-Christian. This has been well demonstrated by E. Kurtz and K. Ketcham in their book, *The Spirituality of Imperfection*. St. Paul, for example, in his Letter to the Romans wrote what an active alcoholic could well say today: "I do not understand my own actions. For I do not do what I want, but I do the very things I hate. . . . I can will what is right, but I cannot do it." Yet Paul saw his powerlessness over "the thorn in my side" as a blessing, for the Lord "said to me 'my grace is sufficient for you, for my power is made perfect in weakness.'" One of A.A.'s original slogans is "But for the grace of God."

And speaking of God's grace, were 12-step spirituality ever to have a patron saint, it would have to be St. Augustine, often referred to as the Doctor of Grace—a writer, philosopher, theologian and a towering figure of his time whose voice is still loud in circles of Christian faiths. His confrontation with heretics was not the greatest battle of his life. It was a battle against addiction.

As a youth Augustine gave full expression to lustful instincts, over which, as he admits in his *Confessions*, he fought a losing battle. "The enemy had control of my will, and from that had made a chain to bind me fast. From a perverted act of will, desire had grown, and when desire is given satisfaction, habit is forged; and when habit passes unresisted, a compulsive urge sets in: by those close-knit links I was held."

Could not anyone truly addicted claim these words as expressing his or her own struggle? Augustine saw that he must, in A.A.'s words, "go to any length" to rid himself of his compulsive urge: "It meant a wholehearted and undivided act of the will, not this stumbling to and fro with a maimed will." Addressing God, he acknowledges that on his own he can do nothing. "The nub of the problem was to reject my own will and to desire yours. . . . What I once feared to lose was now a delight to dismiss." Complete surrender. An *honest* desire, finally.

In the first nine chapters of his *Confessions*, Augustine describes his addiction, its consequences and what took place after his spiritual awakening. It is the self-portrait of a convalescent. This part of the *Confessions*, a Christian classic, is A.A.'s fourth and fifth steps in published form. Augustine saw his confessions as essential to his recovery, admitting his shortcomings to himself, to God and to the people he now served as their bishop, all the while giving God full credit for his recovery.

It was two verses in Paul's Letter to the Romans that turned Augustine's life around: "Let us live honorably in the day, not in reveling and drunkenness, not in debauchery and licentiousness, not in quarreling and jealousy. Instead put on the Lord Jesus Christ, and make no provision for the flesh, to gratify its desires." These were the words Augustine read when he heard a voice telling him to "pick up and read" the Bible.

Of immense help to Catholic recovering alcoholics are local meetings of the Calix Society, which has its headquarters in Minneapolis, Minnesota. Too little known by those Catholics whose lives, except for the grace of God, would have ended in a tragic death, Calix meetings explore with them and their families the riches of their Catholic heritage. Such topics as the workings of grace, the sacraments, God's love and forgiveness are discussed in regard to how these touch upon the participants' ongoing recovery from alcoholism and co-dependency.

In San Diego at the end of June 1995, the bartenders may not have been overjoyed at the huge throng of ex-drinkers who populated the streets of their city. Our contemporary world, however, can well rejoice with the conventioneers in their celebration of the 60-year impact of Alcoholics Anonymous on their lives and those of so many of A.A.'s members, some of whom are prominent citizens. For alcoholism, like any disease, is no respecter of persons.

"The general belief in A.A.'s effectiveness is off the mark."

ALCOHOLICS ANONYMOUS IS INEFFECTIVE

Vince Fox

Vince Fox is a former member of Alcoholics Anonymous (AA). In the following viewpoint, which is excerpted from his book *Addiction, Change and Choice: The New View of Alcoholism*, Fox challenges the commonly held belief that AA is the most effective treatment program for alcoholics. Relatively few problem drinkers become members of AA, according to Fox, and a very small percentage of AA members succeed in staying sober. Fox concludes that various alternatives to AA—including Rational Recovery Systems, Secular Organizations for Sobriety, and Women for Sobriety—are more appropriate than AA for some people.

As you read, consider the following questions:

1. According to Arnold Ludwig, quoted by the author, what percentage of American alcoholics who recover do so using AA?
2. What is the success rate of AA, according to Charles Bufe, as cited by Fox?
3. What has been the result of AA's refusal to acknowledge other treatment programs, in Fox's opinion?

Excerpted from *Addiction, Change, and Choice: The New View of Alcoholism* by Vince Fox. Copyright 1993, 1995 by Vince Fox. Reprinted by permission of See Sharp Press. (Notes/references in the original have been omitted here.)

At a meeting of Alcoholics Anonymous the speaker recommends its program with a ringing declaration, "It works!" True, *but how well does it work?*

Several prestigious organizations seem to know, having endorsed A.A. enthusiastically. Among them are the National Council on Alcoholism and Drug Dependence, the American Medical Association, the American Hospital Association, and the American Association of Addiction Treatment Providers. They certainly ought to know, but do they? Let's take a closer look.

First, is the performance of A.A. commensurate with its reputation? A definitive answer would require facts, but *facts* about A.A. are as scarce as hen's teeth. We can, however, make some judgments by exploring the extent to which A.A.'s members have fulfilled their mission "to stay sober and to help other alcoholics to achieve sobriety." Given the lack of verifiable information from A.A., the question of performance must be referred to scholars and researchers. Is A.A. an effective organization? Here are some answers:

U.S. News and World Report of November 1987 featured an article, "Coming to Grips with Alcoholism," in which it estimated the number of "alcoholics" in the United States at 10.6 million, and A.A. membership at 676,000. That works out to a membership of 6.4% of total potential members. There are extenuating circumstances, of course, but with the benefit of a 52-year nearmonopoly (as of 1987) in its field, that performance—judged by *any* standard—is inadequate.

Of those whom A.A. does reach, the *U.S. News* article continued: ". . . outside researchers—A.A. is reluctant to let them in [!]—believe that perhaps four out of five people who go to A.A. meetings soon drop out." That's a conservative estimate. My opinion is based not only on knowledge gained from years of study and hundreds of contacts, but on personal experience as a former member of A.A. A.A. regulars know about this come-and-go membership problem; they call it A.A.'s "revolving door."

A.A. DOES NOT GET THE JOB DONE

Let us pause to acknowledge the merits of A.A. I've mentioned four approving organizations (there are others), and I know from experience that A.A. is dedicated and conscientious. The question, however, remains: Is it effective? Does it get the job done?

No, says Herbert Fingarette, professor emeritus at the University of California, and former consultant to the United States Supreme Court and the World Health Organization. In his book, *Heavy Drinking*, he states, "It is well known to everyone actively engaged in the field . . . (that) the A.A. program of recovery is simply not acceptable or attractive to the majority of people suffering problems of heavy drinking."

No, says Arnold Ludwig, professor of psychiatry at the University of Kentucky College of Medicine. In his *Understanding the Alcoholic's Mind*, he observes, "Estimates are that only 5 to 10 percent of the alcoholics in this country use A.A. and of those who recover, only 10 percent do so through A.A."

No, says Professor Stanton Peele, social-clinical psychologist and senior survey-researcher at the Mathematical Policy Research Center at Princeton, New Jersey. In his *Diseasing of America: Addiction Treatment Out of Control*, he writes, "In fact, research has not shown A.A. to be an effective treatment for general populations of alcoholics."

No (qualified), says Donald Goodwin, professor and chair of the department of psychiatry at the University of Kansas Medical Center. In his book, *Is Alcoholism Hereditary?*, he observes, "A.A. is credited with helping more alcoholics than all other treatments combined, [but] . . . there is no way of knowing if this is true, since the kind of careful studies needed to show it have not been done."

CONVINCING DATA

No, says Ken Ragge in his *More Revealed: A Critical Analysis of Alcoholics Anonymous and the Twelve Steps*. Ragge devotes a chapter titled "Does It Really Work?" to the question of A.A.'s effectiveness. He references two controlled studies on A.A., both of which produced negative results. He then analyzes the research of psychiatrist George Vaillant of Dartmouth Medical School. Vaillant, author of *The Natural History of Alcoholism*, has produced convincing data indicating that Institutional A.A. is ineffective. Vaillant writes (in "The Doctor's Dilemma"), "The best that can be said for our existing treatment is that we are certainly not interfering with the normal recovery process." Vaillant, however, continues to promote A.A. and the traditional approach in the face of his own research.

No (qualified), says Don Cahalan, professor emeritus of public health at the University of California, Berkeley. In his book, *Understanding America's Drinking Problem*, he states, "It (A.A.) is widely regarded as the most effective avenue for the treatment of alcoholism, although there has been little actual research to bear this out . . . and folklore has it that only about 10 percent of those with the most severe drinking problems ever avail themselves of A.A."

No, says Jerry Dorsman, administrator, researcher, and addictions therapist in Maryland's Cecil County Department of Health,

Division of Mental Health. In his book, *How to Quit Drinking Without A.A.*, he notes, ". . . only 5 to 10 percent of Americans with serious drinking problems belong to A.A. What's worse, among those who join, only about 12% remain in the program more than 3 years." Dorsman does not document his 12% figure, but most researchers would consider his estimate very optimistic.

No, says Jeffrey Schaler, author, editor, and therapist, writing in *Prince George's Journal* of March 1991. He states: "Many people believe that A.A. is the most effective form of treatment for alcoholism. There is no evidence to support this claim."

AA's Membership and Success Rates

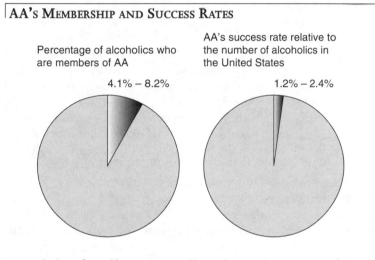

Percentage of alcoholics who are members of AA

4.1% – 8.2%

AA's success rate relative to the number of alcoholics in the United States

1.2% – 2.4%

Source: Charles Bufe, cited by Vince Fox in *Addiction, Change and Choice: The New View of Alcoholism*, 1993.

No, says Charles Bufe in his well-researched *Alcoholics Anonymous: Cult or Cure?* He presents an especially convincing case as follows: An extrapolation from the 1989 membership survey indicates that in that year A.A. claimed 820,000 members in the United States. At that time there were from 10 to 20 million "alcoholics" (by some definition of that nebulous term) in this country. Therefore A.A.'s membership figure represented only 4.1% to 8.2% of the estimated population of alcoholics. Of A.A.'s 820,000 members, the survey asserted that 29% had at least five years sobriety. ("Success" includes length of sobriety, but may not be fully defined by it.) Using A.A.'s 29% figure as a criterion of success, Bufe calculated an overall success rate of 1.2% to 2.4% relative to the number of alcoholics in the United States, and he went on to estimate that A.A.'s success rate relative to past and present members is at most 2.4% to 4.8%.

Bufe estimates that 50% to 90% of all heavy drinkers investigate A.A. at some time during their drinking careers; this by virtue of the facts that: 1) A.A. is a mandatory part of treatment in 99% of treatment centers; 2) drunk drivers and other alcoholic offenders are routinely sentenced to A.A. in most parts of the country; and 3) the general *perceptions*, popular and professional, that A.A. is successful and that it's the only program available to problem drinkers, results in a large amount of "walk-in traffic" for A.A.

My own position is that the general belief in A.A.'s effectiveness is off the mark. . . .

INADVERTENT HOMICIDE

The root cause of A.A.'s problems lies in its myopic views and in what may be termed a "meanness of spirit." A.A. may, in truth, even be guilty of a kind of inadvertent homicide, practiced in the name of its conviction that it is the *way*—the one and only way—whereby an alcoholic can achieve sobriety and the good life. That statement is less than a formal charge, but more than a literary device. Please walk for a moment in the shoes of those who entered, then exited, the "revolving doors" of A.A.

Most of them came freely and heroically to face the problem at last. They were welcomed warmly and accepted without judgment, and, for a while, were at peace. But soon came a disturbing awareness of an incompatibility between many of their convictions, values, and beliefs, and the tenets of the A.A. program. In moments of discontent they wondered aloud and were told "Some people are too smart to make it in A.A.," or "Take the cotton out of your ears and put it in your mouth," or "Let go and let God." Translation: Don't think, believe, and let God and A.A. do it for you. But no one said, "Hey, if our program doesn't fit your needs, let me tell you about some others that might. There *are* eight others, you know." They said, instead, "Keep coming back."

A.A. knows that other self-help support programs exist, but refuses to acknowledge them even when its members ask about alternatives. A.A.'s unwavering response to such queries is to advise questioners to read the Big Book, go to meetings, and "keep coming back." That's not an answer: it's a refusal to answer. A.A. purports to cooperate but not affiliate, and does neither. To pretend ignorance of other programs in the face of a direct question, or to refuse to impart known information, is not only dishonest but often damaging to thousands of people in need.

Ignorance of alternative programs is no excuse; only a recent arrival from the planet Zenobica could be ignorant of the fact that there are many programs now available to alcoholics. . . .

Over the years, hundreds of thousands of heavy drinkers have found A.A. unsuited to their needs and alien to their values. They sought other avenues of recovery, and pioneers such as Jack Trimpey of Rational Recovery and Jean Kirkpatrick of Women for Sobriety established national organizations to meet those needs. These organizations and six others are widely established throughout the United States and in several other countries. Their books are in most public libraries, and hundreds of articles have appeared about them in newspapers and magazines across the country (*The New York Times*, *The Washington Post*, *Newsweek*, *Reason*, and many others).

A LACK OF COMPASSION

Yet, to those who ask and are in need, A.A. remains inflexible, mute, and uncooperative, like the lonely king in *The Little Prince* who still "ruled" a world of his own making, oblivious to everything but his own kingdom. The A.A. "king"—its General Service Board—continues to maintain a position that reflects a serious lack of understanding and compassion for those who have tried its program, found it unsuitable to their needs, and are in search of an alternative. As a former victim of this policy, I remain affronted by it in the name of millions harmed by it. That's a polite way of saying that I'm damned well ticked off about it. A.A. is acting in a seriously unethical manner by withholding vital—*as in life and death*—information. The prevailing A.A. policy displays a lack of compassion, honesty, courtesy, and simple decency.

As a result of this rigid policy, countless individuals have left A.A. They left in despair and desperation, weary and worried, wondering what to do next, having played and lost at what they thought was the only game in town. They staggered away toward an empty life, the loneliness of a crowded tavern, a lost job, a failed marriage, an institution, and—sometimes—a cemetery. Their explanations? "The program just didn't work for me," or "I couldn't handle all that God-stuff." And often they protested, "Hell, I'm not *powerless*, and I'm certainly not *diseased!*, and I'm not about to go to meetings for the rest of my life. I just drink too much."

Those are *objections*, not excuses—words of frustration, not of criticism. It's baffling; A.A. is not, for the most part, filled with mean and mindless people, so why this tone of self-righteous fundamentalism, this "My way or the highway" position? Part of the answer lies in A.A.'s hallowed Traditions, rudders that guided A.A. during its early years. But in time those rudders have become anchors. And now they are virtual laws, helpful to some but hurtful to many.

Another part of the answer lies in the abandonment of [A.A. cofounder] Bill Wilson's position on alternative therapies by A.A.'s GSO [General Service Office] and Board. It was Wilson who said, "Upon therapy for the alcoholic himself, we surely have no monopoly." He would have agreed with a recent statement by Dr. Robert Sparks, president emeritus and senior consultant to the W.K. Kellogg Foundation. The Institute of Medicine of the National Academy of Sciences appointed Sparks to lead a special investigative group devoted to the study of alcohol treatment problems. Speaking for that committee, Sparks said, ". . . no single approach works for everybody. . . . The challenge is to match the individuals with the right programs." He praised A.A., then added, "Yet, A.A. is not for everyone." Bill Wilson would have approved; A.A.'s General Service Board would not. The membership seems ambivalent; at meetings one hears "We're not for everybody" and "It's our way or the highway."

A Veritable Antique

A.A.'s uncompromising position can be explained in yet another way: change is painful, but when an idea becomes fixed and institutionalized, change becomes not just painful but excruciating, and is often postponed indefinitely. Hence, no change. In increasing numbers, legions of the New Guard look upon A.A. of today with an impatience tinged with anger, tempered by sadness. They regard it as a product of the 1930s, encapsulated in a cocoon, time-warped into a new world, impervious to substantive change, even resistant to survival-sustaining adaptation. A.A., the courageous pioneer of the thirties, became a quaint anachronism by the 1960s and is a veritable antique in the 1990s. It still works, as a Model A Ford "works," but not very well on an eight-lane super highway.

That may help to explain the provincialism of many of A.A.'s adherents, but is of no help to those thousands of disheartened and disillusioned people who, when they departed A.A., resigned themselves to despair, and were labeled failures. Failures? No. Absolutely not! They had not failed A.A.—A.A. had failed them. They could not bend far enough, and A.A. would not bend at all. They had come, seen, and left unconquered, but many were bruised and others broken by a rigidity intended as a kindness.

A.A. has filled a small niche, and left a large void.

That void is now being filled by eight self-help programs for those with problems associated with drinking, drugging, or both. Three of these groups are A.A.-type quasi-clones (Calix, JACS [Jewish Alcoholics, Chemically Dependent Persons and Significant Others Foundation], and AV [Alcoholics Victorious]), one of them (SOS [Secular Organizations for Sobriety]) defies classification, and four of them are true independents which are basically antithetical to A.A., and divergent from it in both theory and practice. All of them are designed to fill major areas of need such as those of atheists, casual Christians, Jews, women, non-theists, nominal Catholics, humanists, et al. Three of them have emerged as major players: Rational Recovery Systems, Women for Sobriety, and Secular Organizations for Sobriety. They, and the others, exist for the same reason that shoes are made in different sizes.

"[The SOS 'program'] will help you achieve and maintain a lasting, continual abstinence-freedom from alcohol and drug dependency."

SECULAR ORGANIZATIONS FOR SOBRIETY IS AN EFFECTIVE SELF-HELP PROGRAM

James Christopher

Secular Organizations for Sobriety (SOS), also known as Save Our Selves, was created by James Christopher as a secular alternative to Alcoholics Anonymous (AA). In the following viewpoint, which is written in a question-and-answer format, Christopher explains that instead of climbing a series of spiritual steps, alcoholics in SOS make a rational choice to establish sobriety as "Priority One." SOS is an effective option for alcoholics who are unable to benefit from AA's emphasis on spirituality, according to Christopher. Christopher is the author of several books, including *SOS Sobriety: The Proven Alternative to Twelve-Step Programs*, from which this viewpoint is excerpted.

As you read, consider the following questions:

1. What are the three elements of the cycle of addiction, as described by Christopher? What are the three elements of the cycle of recovery?
2. According to the author, why is the original reason for an alcoholic's drinking irrelevant to his or her recovery process?
3. In what ways have treatment center professionals responded to SOS, according to Christopher?

Q: What is alcoholism, anyway?

A: The jury is still out. Personally, I'm impressed by the reams of research data that show some folks (about 10 percent of this country's populace) become physiologically hooked on booze at the cellular level, experiencing (over time) problems in their lives directly attributed to ingesting the drug alcohol. Incidentally, I've never met anyone who intended to get hooked on alcohol or any other drug. Other people, i.e., nonalcoholics, seem to be able to drink as they choose, when they choose, with impunity. Some of us seem to be predestined to cellular addiction via genetics; some researchers also include the possibility that any drinker—who consumes alcohol long enough and hard enough—may eventually join the "cellular addiction crowd." This means that one's primitive limbic system, or the "lizard brain," that knows only its need, receives an alcohol = pleasure imprint with each sip of booze, regardless of the next morning's hangover, smashed car, or wrecked life. Most SOS members are comfortable with viewing alcoholism as both a progressive disease process and a habit, but SOS meetings offer a "freethought forum for recovery." Therefore, if anyone were to attend an SOS meeting expressing a desire to achieve and maintain sobriety (abstinence) by a different pathway, he or she would be welcome. Even if a person stated that he or she stayed sober by jumping on a trampoline twice a day, he or she would be welcomed.

Q: That's cute, but what about those persons who wish to learn to control and enjoy their drinking? Does SOS accommodate them?

A: No. Their needs would be better served elsewhere. Our name says it all: *Secular Organizations for Sobriety* and *Save Our Selves*. We're an *abstinence* group. Anyone sincerely seeking sobriety in a secular setting is welcome. . . .

Q: What is the SOS program of recovery?

A: The SOS "program" is offered as a suggested strategy. It will help you achieve and maintain a lasting, continual abstinence-freedom from alcohol and drug dependency. Persons grappling with issues other than alcoholism (overeaters, gamblers, etc.) have successfully utilized the SOS approach as well. Here's the essence of the SOS program.

THE CYCLE OF ADDICTION

The Sobriety Priority approach for achieving and maintaining freedom from alcohol and other mind-altering drugs is a *cognitive* strategy. It can be applied on a daily basis to prevent relapse as long as one lives.

The Sobriety Priority approach respects the power of "nature" (genetic inheritance, progressive disease processes) and of "nurture" (learned habit, behaviors, and associations) by showing how to achieve the initial arrest of cellular addiction and stave off the chronic habits that result from this addiction.

The "cycle of addiction" contains three debilitating elements: chemical need (at the physiological cellular level), learned habit (chronic, drinking/using behaviors and associations), and denial of both need and habit.

The cycle of alcohol addiction usually develops over a period of years. Cycles have been found to be much shorter with other drugs, especially cocaine. In all cases, however, the addiction becomes "Priority One," a separate issue from everything else. And as the addiction progresses, it begins to negate everything else.

The Cycle of Sobriety

The cycle of addiction can be successfully replaced by another cycle: the cycle of sobriety. This cycle contains three essential elements: acknowledgment of one's addiction to alcohol or drugs (perhaps once euphemistically called "a problem"), acceptance of one's disease/habit, and prioritization of sobriety as the primary issue in one's life.

The daily cognitive application of a new "Priority One," the Sobriety Priority, as a separate issue arrests the cycle of addiction. It frees the sober alcoholic/addict to experience "everything else" by teaching him or her to associate "everything else" with sobriety, not with drinking or using behaviors. The cycle of sobriety remains in place only so long as the sober alcoholic/addict cognitively chooses to continue to acknowledge the existence of his or her alcoholism or drug addiction.

The Sobriety Priority, applied daily, gradually weakens booze and drug associations, halting the cycle of addiction and allowing time for new associations to form as one experiences life without addictive chemicals. As one continues to "make peace" with the facts regarding his or her arrested addiction—that is, as one continues to recognize alcohol and/or drugs as nonoptions—one comes to prefer a sober lifestyle: one longs to preserve it, to respect the arrested chemical addiction, and to protect the new, sober life.

Q: Is SOS, then, focusing on achieving and maintaining sobriety (i.e., abstinence) rather than a "wholistic" recovery?

A: Yes. SOS members can utilize "the sobriety priority" as a separate issue from all else, so that in sobriety they are then "freed up" to address their other life issues.

Q: Yes, but where's the "program" as it pertains to a plan for living?

A: The Sobriety Priority, accepted and maintained as a separate issue, empowers one to choose his or her own plan or design for living, regardless of one's unresolved life issues. *We deliberately offer no quality-of-life program: We do not tell each other how to live.* Consequently, we eschew sponsorship (the AA "buddy system") because it has been shown to foster "guruism." Instead, we approach each other as equals, respecting our diversity.

SURVIVAL IS AT STAKE

Q: What about one's reasons for drinking in the first place? How is that addressed?

A: Research has shown that alcoholics and nonalcoholics drink for the same reasons. Some will get hooked, others will not (so much for the "alcoholic personality" theories). One's original reasons for drinking may have dissipated over time or may remain in full force. But, if one has acknowledged and accepted the fact that one cannot drink and get away with it, and if one maintains awareness of that fact as a required life-and-death necessity, one has no real choice. Therefore, drinking is not an option when one's survival is seriously threatened. I cannot escape life's challenges by walking in front of an oncoming bus without paying the ultimate price—i.e., I cannot walk in front of an oncoming bus and get away with it. My "lizard brain" or limbic system reacts instantly to "flight or fight"/"do or don't" survival situations.

A SAFE AND RICH ENVIRONMENT

SOS for me has not been a ready-made off-the-shelf treatment program, but rather a safe and rich environment in which I could devise a treatment for my own self. Safe, because I have learned in these meetings that no matter what I say and reveal about my inner hurts, no harm will come to me. Rich, because by listening to the other participants and reading the literature, I have available to me a wealth of insights, tools and methods for overcoming my enemy within, and for leading a sober life.

Marty N., *SOS International Newsletter*, Fall 1996.

Sips of alcohol imprint on the limbic system as instantaneous pleasure, not pain. Sticking one's hand in a flame imprints as instantaneous pain. So one automatically avoids this behavior in the future. Alcohol avoidance can become immediate if a person accepts that alcohol literally threatens his or her survival. A person's recognition of his or her survival needs thereby can compensate for that person's natural selective memory and negate denial. Rather than resolving issues that may have been one's original reason(s) to drink, rather than attempting to live in a certain way to avoid certain human emotions or circumstances any human being is likely to experience, one can choose to stay sober and to avoid alcohol "no matter what"—*because no reason in the universe exists for a drink if one acknowledges and accepts that it threatens one's very survival.* For alcoholics drink = pain, or drink = death. Survival is at stake. Therefore, limbic system lies are challenged by passionate realizations of truth: "My name is Jim. I am a sober alcoholic. I cannot and do not drink no matter what, because I cannot drink and get away with it." This is not a statement about my "character." Rather, it is an acknowledgement and acceptance of truth regarding me, physiologically, chemically. *A separate issue.* My survival depends upon it. . . .

GETTING BUSY

Q: How are SOS meetings conducted? What happens? What are the "healing dynamics" within this "freethought forum in recovery"?

A: I contend that the very act of people sharing together is an acknowledgement of one's situation. Bolstered by the empathic support of one's peers, freethought-forum, egalitarian self-help groups can be "dynamite" in positive effectiveness! When your meeting format provides a focus, factoring out rigid controls (and controllers), "spiritual" or secular, you can really get somewhere. You can experience positive change and growth. . . .

Q: What happens to SOS members? Do they have to attend SOS for the rest of their lives? What happens in the SOS version of recovery?

A: As an abstinence movement, SOS offers a freethought forum providing an informal support system for recovery. All persons grow at their own pace. SOS members share in confidence with each other their separate-issue life challenges. Some folks initially attend some SOS meetings and then choose to attend no longer, preferring a "private recovery," if you will. Research has shown that many persons achieve a "clean and sober" lifestyle without support of any kind. Their recovery, as is the recovery of those in AA, Women for Sobriety, etc., is as valid as anyone else's recovery.

SOS members tend to view SOS meetings as an awareness tool. Most do not "play out their lives" in daily meetings of any kind. Since we credit ourselves for our achievement and maintenance of sobriety, most of us utilize the "citizens of the world" concept; i.e., we get on with our lives as clean and sober alcoholics/addicts, while continuing to take full advantage of SOS group support and to feel good from altruistically giving back support to those new to recovery. Although some persons get sober and sit on the bleachers of life, scarfing down donuts and gallons of caffeinated coffee laced with refined sugar, chain-smoking cigarettes, and being generally complacent—except about the individual sobriety priority—many others opt for the engagé position, at least to some extent. Arsenio Hall, a popular television talk show host, might say that "We get busy!"

There's lots going on in life beyond drinking and drugging! . . .

TREATMENT PROFESSIONALS AND SOS

Q: How have chemical dependency treatment professionals, referral agencies, and the courts viewed the advent of SOS?

A: Since 1987, Los Angeles courts have given persons mandated to attend abstinence support groups a choice between AA and SOS. As they've learned about SOS, many other courts across the country have followed suit, pleased to have an additional option. Thousands of members of the helping professions—physicians, psychologists, psychiatrists, professional counselors, nurses, chemical dependency treatment professionals, as well as related referral agencies—have happily utilized SOS groups as a viable recovery alternative for their patients and clients. The climate is changing in the recovery field. . . .

Treatment center professionals have been both mean-spirited and open-minded. A recent incident is indeed heartening and has been repeated in treatment facilities nationwide. The program director of a major treatment center in New York State, familiar with SOS and open to options in recovery, invited a local SOS group to hold meetings in the treatment facility on an open basis (both patients and outsiders in recovery were welcome). At first, this action was met with objections from 12-stepping treatment personnel. As time passed and patients in sufficient numbers who had not been comfortable with AA responded dramatically to treatment, the same 12-step adherents came to the program director, apologizing and acknowledging that without the SOS option a significant number of patients would not have had an effective recovery experience in treatment.

Recently, an extremely distraught psychologist, in practice for many years, called the SOS Clearinghouse conveying that his daughter and son were hooked on drugs. He said that he realized alcoholism and other drug addictions had to be approached as the priority and as a separate issue, not as a psychological "symptom." Both siblings had almost died; they had not fared well with the AA approach. SOS assisted him in finding a treatment center that was open to options. This sort of thing happens all too frequently, but change is here.

Schick Shadel Hospitals, for example, offer medical synchrotherapy (aversion treatment), AA, and also other options, respecting personal philosophies both in treatment and in aftercare. Unfortunately, Schick Hospitals are only available in three states: California, Texas, and Washington. Heretofore, AA was pushed as the only way to recovery in virtually all inpatient and outpatient treatment facilities. Certified alcoholism counselors (often 12-step zealots) told their charges: "If you don't accept the AA philosophy, you will die out there." This is obviously not true, and these attitudes have to some extent mercifully changed.

SOS is not in competition with any group. In offering a way, and a freethought-forum approach, we're positively thrilled with folks finding recovery—any recovery—however it's achieved! . . .

HOPES FOR THE FUTURE

Q: What are your personal hopes for SOS in the future? How do you think "recovery methods" and related research will evolve to address rampant global alcohol- and drug-addiction problems?

A: I hope SOS will thrive as a friendly alternative, one of many abstinence-based approaches that, I hope, will emerge in the not-too-distant future.

Although my personal sobriety is not dependent on the continuing existence of SOS—and that's the general viewpoint of SOS members regarding dependency on any group—SOS fills a need, as evidenced by its rapid growth in the [first] five years of its existence. I hope AA and other 12-step abstinence groups will continue to flourish, and that AA will eventually update its precepts while still honoring its roots and those very dedicated pioneers who originated it.

We already see evidence that research validates the SOS "separate-issue" approach. We human beings are chemical creatures. We'll know much more in ten or twenty years, but, for now, we can work together as allies in recovery and research, utilizing the scientific method as well as compassion in that process.

| "Rational Recovery ... is a pioneering effort to bring order to the chaotic addictions field."

RATIONAL RECOVERY IS AN EFFECTIVE SELF-HELP PROGRAM

Jack Trimpey

Rational Recovery (RR) is a network of self-help groups founded by Jack Trimpey. In the following viewpoint, Trimpey explains how his dissatisfaction with Alcoholics Anonymous (AA) led him to create RR. Rejecting AA's view that alcoholism is a disease over which the alcoholic is powerless, Trimpey insists that alcoholics can stop drinking whenever they choose to. According to Trimpey, RR helps alcoholics quit drinking by means of a thinking skill called Addictive Voice Recognition Technique (AVRT), which involves recognizing and defeating the internal voice that urges one to drink. Trimpey is the author of *The Small Book* and *Rational Recovery: The New Cure for Substance Addiction*, from which this viewpoint is excerpted.

As you read, consider the following questions:

1. According to Trimpey, how does his conception of God differ from AA's conception of God?
2. What percentage of those who recover from serious addiction do so without getting help, according to the author?
3. Out of the group of 250 AVRT enrollees mentioned by the author, what percentage remain abstinent?

O ver a decade ago, I defeated my own twenty-year addiction to alcohol by stubbornly refusing to drink any more of it. I had struggled with alcohol dependence for many years, enjoying its pleasure and suffering its sting, convinced all the while that I was somehow "marked" to continue my folly. I thought I had a disease that caused me to drink against my own better judgment.

As a professional social worker in the 1970s and later, I actively promoted the popular belief that alcoholism is a *disease*, probably inherited, certainly incurable, and one that renders a person powerless over the choice to drink or not. I referred all of the problem drinkers ("alcoholics") I saw to the 12-step program of Alcoholics Anonymous (AA), which for many years has enjoyed a reputation as the only thing that really works. I noticed that very few who attended AA really stopped drinking, but I thought, "I understand their problem because I have it, too. I can see why they don't get better." I was strangely fascinated that "we alcoholics" continue to drink in spite of the well-known trajectory to despair that lies ahead. I did not suspect until much later that it was partly *because* of the popular disease concept that so many fulfill its sodden promise.

ENCOUNTERING AA

Since my early twenties, I had been a world-class drinker, far outdoing others I knew in the pursuit of alcoholic pleasures. I did not attend very many AA meetings myself, perhaps thirty in all, because AA's 12-step program made little sense to me. Also, I am not group-oriented. I am not inclined to talk about my personal problems in front of strangers. I began attending AA meetings in the late 1960s. I was in my late twenties, having a rip-roaring time getting drunk in the evenings and weekends, and sometimes I went to work recovering from hangovers. My tolerant boss once noted on a performance evaluation, "He comes to work with the residuals of the night before." Undeterred, I continued drinking with the idea of being more careful in the future. One late night I wrecked the family car while under the influence of alcohol. My wife, Lois, finally demanded that I do something about the problem, and she took me to an AA meeting held in a church basement. I went inside.

On a coffee table, illuminated by a candle, the Holy Bible was lying open. I listened as a group of gaunt, unshaven men told of their sad experiences in life and spoke reverently of "the program." Gesturing toward the 12-step creed hanging on the wall, one of them told me that I could survive the deadly disease of alcoholism by joining their "fellowship." I cringed a little, but I drew upon my humility (actually my fear of getting fired from my job and being divorced) to listen further.

They described their fellowship as "not religious but spiritual," but I immediately recognized that their program of twelve steps was distinctly and intensely religious. I found this puzzling because I have always viewed religion as something to be held out for the world to see, even to be proud of, certainly not to be hidden or disguised as something else. I wondered why they would say their program wasn't religious when it obviously was. . . .

This was not adding up. I thought I had come to a meeting of former drinkers who would explain to me how they quit drinking. I fully expected that they would inspire me to knock it off, to help me grin and bear the difficulties of quitting, and perhaps to offer me some encouragement when I felt tempted to drink. I already sensed that sooner or later my drinking would have to come to a halt. Later, of course, sounded much better than sooner. I later learned that "halt" had another meaning in AA, that the letters h-a-l-t stood for *hungry, angry, lonely,* and *tired*—four daily-occurring conditions under which the Fellowship predicts people will drink alcohol unless they are "working a good program."

THE RELIGION OF AA

My perception that AA was religious was confirmed when I read "The Big Book." As a well-churched person, I had read that kind of material for many years. I commented on this at a meeting, and someone explained that religions are not geared to handle alcoholism, that alcoholic priests and ministers come to AA because they need more than their religions can provide. Someone else chimed in to reassure everyone that AA is nevertheless compatible with all religions, ". . . and in fact, AA has salvaged many from alcoholism and sent them back to become upstanding members of their churches."

I accepted this explanation, not only because I had more pressing concerns than to debate the matter, but because I did not feel like challenging this group of sincere, well-meaning people who, it would seem, knew more about alcoholism than I did and who agreed with each other on absolutely everything. "Take what you like and leave the rest," they said, so that is what I did.

I eventually left the religious 12 steps, each of them, but took the disease concept as my own. The disease idea clicked profoundly within me. The moment I thought of drinking as a symptom of a disease I had probably inherited, it felt as if a great responsibility had been lifted from my shoulders. My guts settled down, and I could suddenly see my own behavior in a different light. No longer did it seem that I was behaving stupidly and irresponsibly, no longer did I sense an urgent need to quit drinking alcohol, and no longer did it make sense for me to damn myself for my behavior. I was simply doing what we alcoholics do. We eat to live and live to drink, knowing that tomorrow we may die. . . .

GOD AS AA UNDERSTANDS HIM

Although I expected that something would eventually have to intervene or rescue me, I could not imagine anything that could prevent me—or even *deter* me—from drinking. As a child growing up in the Methodist Church, I learned to worship and pray to God, but not to expect favors from God. My God cannot be manipulated, does no favors, doesn't disappoint, and doesn't get even. Aloof from human affairs, my God is simply recognized, honored, or worshipped in a spiritual way. He's just there, and that's that.

As AA understands Him, however, God was going to live my life for me, take control of me, provide character repairs, and miraculously keep me sober. This was out of the question. I would live free or die.

When I explained my personal beliefs to the group, they told me to read "The Big Book." I reread it, and I was once again insulted by its sophomoric fundamentalism and even more concerned that AA claimed to surpass the great religions of the world in its ability to contend with addiction.

I got the message clearly: If I didn't surrender my critical judgment, my personal beliefs, and my *self* to the Fellowship of AA, I was doomed to drink myself to jail, to asylums, to hospitals, and to death. "Anything can be your Higher Power. Try nature," one AAer said. So I tried nature as my HP. But my appreciation of nature in those days was *heightened* by a few drinks—I drank to brighten the sunrise and to beautify the sunset. "Try wisdom," another AAer coached. So I tried wisdom as my HP, and I found that I did not have the wisdom to know wisdom from folly. "Then," they said, "let the AA group be your Higher Power," and I looked around the room and saw a group of people I would not choose as friends who were willing to pose as my God. They finally said, "Well then, you can be your own Higher Power." I then knew that something had happened to them and they were no longer thinking for themselves, that their spiritual program was more important to them than common sense, or my problem. I tried a number of HP's, theirs and mine, and they all turned out to be flops at keeping me sober.

LOVING THE DISEASE

"You just want to drink. You aren't ready to quit," they finally said. I knew I wanted to quit, but I also knew they were right. They told me that if I didn't turn my life over to a Higher Power, I would continue to drink. When I suggested I would quit on my own, they said that would be impossible, and even if I did quit for a while, I could not be happy and would eventually relapse. "You are in denial," they said, "which is a symptom of your disease."

Part of me wanted to agree with them. That "part of me" was never discussed in AA. It was simply called an incurable disease. I loved my disease for reasons I did not know, so I accepted that I was crazy to think I could stop drinking all on my own.

I tried a number of different AA groups in different cities, seeking one with a different flavor. There was one called "We Agnostics," to which the mainstream groups sent their "intellectuals, atheists, and agnostics." There, members found support since they were with their own kind, a subspecies of alcoholic seemingly unfit for the regular simple program of spiritual nourishment. Few noticed or seemed to care that there was no written program to replace the standard 12-step program, and that an entire chapter of "The Big Book" was devoted to predicting the demise of agnostics, atheists, and intellectuals. Several ersatz versions of the 12 steps were circulated, with objectionable words and phrases whited out or paraphrased. There was some effort to use current psychological theories to bolster the down-home religious concepts such as taking moral inventories and making amends, but in the final analysis, these maverick groups were identical to the main groups. They were convinced that they suffered a disease that made them different from others, and they believed that if they did not attend recovery group meetings, they would inevitably fall off the wagon.

I quit AA and continued to drink for many more years, as they predicted. I thought they were crazy on the one hand, but quite right on the other. I continued with my career as a social worker, fairly steadily during the days, and often drank during evenings and weekends. As a social worker, I was well placed to search for special programs that might be more relevant, and I did check around, but AA was the only game in town. I attended meetings sporadically with the idea that maybe something, either AA or I, might have changed.

Neither ever did. Looking back, I can see that many of my perceptions were shaped by society at large, which has embraced a philosophy of addiction that *fosters* addiction. I also see that my original, natural viewpoint, before my exposure to professional education and 12-step meeting attendance, was right on target: Anyone can quit now for good, and I had better bite the bullet and get my recovery over with. I had learned the value of individual responsibility as a child, but as an adult I surrendered to a highly gratifying belief that I drank for hidden causes and would need outside help of some kind to stop.

QUITTING FOR GOOD

Finally, around 1982, when I had had enough (problems, not alcohol), I decided that either AA was essentially right or AA was essentially wrong. If AA was correct, I reasoned, I would soon die. If AA was dead wrong, as I had long suspected, then I was solely responsible to take control and quit drinking altogether. I finally picked a time, and when that time came, I did it.

Quitting for good was much easier than I thought. When I decided I would no longer drink, I resumed my life—as a person who simply does not drink alcohol. The first couple of months were the most difficult, with much yearning to drink and some irritability, but I did not become like an adolescent, as predicted by experts who believe that addicted people do not grow and mature. Few besides my family even noticed. Because normal behavior is so unremarkable, even *they* soon began taking my abstinence for granted.

Before long, I was feeling much better and enjoying life. For a couple of years, however, I noticed that I still felt insecure about the possibility of relapse. Occasionally, Lois would imagine I was off somewhere drinking. I wondered, "What if AA is right? What if it is true that I cannot do it on my own? Maybe I'm just a dry drunk, biding my time until my next downfall?" I considered returning to AA for a "tune-up," to see if I could fit in sober, as a way to reinforce my plan to stay sober.

I didn't return to AA because it finally dawned on me that Lois had been right all along, that I had made myself physically dependent on alcohol by drinking so much of it, that I had sustained my addiction by avoiding my own responsibility to stop, and that I had continued drinking in spite of the bad consequences because I accepted the *nonsensical* idea that I was powerless to do otherwise. My attachment to my "disease-of-relapse" (as alcoholism is often referred to) was simply a respectable way of planning to drink in the future.

When it finally sank in after two years that I would never drink under any circumstances and that I could predict this with a high level of confidence, my addiction was over. I could finally see myself as a normal, healthy human being who simply doesn't drink alcohol. At first I thought I had accomplished something very special, that I had beat the high odds against me.

AVRT BRIEFLY DESCRIBED

Observe your thoughts and feelings, positive and negative, about drinking or using. Thoughts and feelings that support continued use are called the Addictive Voice (AV); those that support abstinence are you. When you recognize and understand your AV, it becomes not-you, but "it," an easily defeated enemy that has been causing you to drink. All it wants is pleasure. "I want a drink" becomes "It wants a drink." Think to yourself, "I will never drink again," and listen for its reaction. Your negative thoughts and feelings are your AV talking back to you. Now, think, "I will drink/use whenever I please." Your pleasant feelings are also the AV, which is in control. Recovery is not a process; it is an event. The magic word is "Never," as in, "I will never drink/use again." Recognition defeats short-term desire, and abstinence soon becomes effortless. Complete separation of "you" from "it" leads to complete recovery and hope for a better life. The only time you can drink is now, and the only time you can quit for good is right now. "I will never drink/use again" becomes "I never drink now." It's not hard; anyone can do it.

Jack Trimpey, *Rational Recovery: The New Cure for Substance Addiction*, 1996.

I now know that self-recovery such as mine is commonplace. According to research, fully 40% to 70% of those who recover from serious addictions do so without getting help of any kind, including attending self-help and support groups. People do it all the time, but they are dismissed as "not really alcoholic." To follow this logic, no one is an "alcoholic" until they attend their first AA meeting.

THE BIRTH OF RATIONAL RECOVERY

Working at a county mental health clinic, I came across many people who wanted to quit drinking but nevertheless continued. . . .

One day, I called every hospital within two hundred miles asking what services existed for people who did not want to participate in a 12-step program. I found none. The people I spoke to said, "No other program works. AA is broad enough for all people. People who don't want to participate in a 12-step program aren't really motivated. Some people have to get worse before they get better."

Lois and I talked often about the 12-step monopoly, sometimes late into the night, and our fascination and interest grew. In 1985, we decided to work together during our free time (Lois was a high school teacher) to create a new organization, patterned after AA but emphasizing abstinence through self-reliance and common sense. We settled on the name "Rational Recovery." We ran a few ads in magazines and newspapers, and soon we started hearing from addicted people and their relatives from all over the nation who were undertaking the same search. They, too, had found that all roads to help lead to the 12-step program of AA—it was the only recovery game throughout America.

I decided to go to bat for people who simply wanted to recover from their addictions by using their own natural abilities. In 1986, I started several Rational Recovery self-help groups in the Central Valley of California, and people attended in increasing numbers.

I found there was a complete absence of self-help literature that did not promote the "disease thinking" of AA, so to give participants something to work with, I wrote a series of essays for the group. Many of them noticed that my material contradicted most of what was set forth in *The Big Book*. One evening, Lois suggested the essays could be organized into a small book called *The Small Book*, and within two years *The Small Book* became a groundbreaking publication in the addictions field. . . .

The Small Book sets forth concepts of Addictive Voice Recognition Technique, or AVRT, provides a backdrop of psychological self-help material, and presents what is probably the first step-by-step critique of the 12-step program of AA in print. It has been used for years as a central reference for RRSN [Rational Recovery Self-Help Network] participants, and it is widely used to define and characterize Rational Recovery. *The Small Book* continues to be recognized as a groundbreaking publication in the addictions field and is a valuable guide for people emerging from AA and addiction "treatment.". . .

A PIONEERING EFFORT

Rational Recovery, now over a decade old, is a pioneering effort to bring order to the chaotic addictions field. Along the way, we have learned many things we did not expect to learn, such as the surprising potency of AVRT, which has shaped our program.

Of a group of 250 persons who enrolled in AVRT: The Course

between 1991 and 1993, 65% remain abstinent today. All had extensive unsuccessful experiences in AA and about 90% had multiple prior admissions to 12-step treatment programs. A study of Rational Recovery self-help groups by New York University Medical School at Bellevue Hospital conducted by Marc Galanter, M.D. ("Rational Recovery: An Alternative to AA for Addiction," *The American Journal of Drug and Alcohol Abuse*, 19:4, 1993, pp. 499–510), found that 74% of those who attended for four months were abstinent. Approximately 300 early responses to a questionnaire at the back of *The Small Book* immediately following publication of the book found 91% abstinent, not surprising for a self-selected population, but nevertheless an indicator that something very good is going on.

| "Men on naltrexone reported less craving for alcohol, and fewer days on which they drank."

MEDICATION MAY HELP ALCOHOLICS STAY SOBER

David Brown

In the following viewpoint, *Washington Post* staff writer David Brown reports that researchers have made progress toward under-standing how alcohol affects the brain and how these effects can lead to addiction. With this knowledge, he writes, scientists have begun to develop drugs to treat alcoholics. Brown cautions that these drugs have shown only slight promise so far and that alcohol dependency is too complex to be cured with a "magic bullet." However, he states that one drug—naltrexone—has had positive results, an encouraging step in the effort to combat alcoholism.

As you read, consider the following questions:

1. How does the effect of alcohol on the brain differ from that of heroin, according to Brown?
2. What surprising result of the Yale study underscores the complexity of alcoholism, in the author's opinion?

For both alcoholics and the people who'd like to help them, it might be easier if alcohol were a little more like heroin. Heroin is a complex biochemical that finds a home in only very specific places of the brain and spinal cord. It fits into the so-called opiate receptors of cells, like a key in a lock. Though almost nothing in the human nervous system is straightforward, at least this first step of heroin's myriad effects is simple.

A PRIMITIVE DRUG

Alcohol, however, is something else. This oldest of human intoxicants is also, in many ways, the most primitive. It has no receptor. It doesn't do anything as elegant as find its own keyhole in the cell's many doors of perception.

Instead, alcohol insinuates itself into countless parts of the cell. One of the things it seems especially able to do is disrupt the molecules of water that coat and scaffold the proteins that make up receptors. It does this at some receptors after two beers, at others only when the receptors' owner is heading toward staggering drunk. Alcohol makes some of these receptors more sensitive—it turns them on. Others it switches off. Each action, in turn, sets in motion complicated changes in the "downstream" circuitry of the brain.

All in all, this makes alcohol's influence more complex, probably, than any other substance mankind is wont to abuse.

PROGRESS

Neuroscientists in the past two decades have made substantial progress in learning the immediate mechanics of alcohol's activity as well as its more indirect effects. These insights, in turn, have led to experiments in which drugs with specific receptor-based function are given to abstinent alcoholics in an effort to keep them from returning to drink.

The drugs studied so far as treatments for alcoholism are only a little help, if that. (Personal choice and motivation will always be the essential ingredients for abstinence.) Nevertheless, with about 15 million people meeting psychiatry's definition of alcohol abuse or dependence, researchers believe that even a little help may be worth it.

It is now clear that much of alcohol's action occurs along an anatomical loop that begins in the brain stem, a structure between the spinal cord and the brain that is seat to many essential, though unconscious, functions. The nerve cells, or neurons, there send connections to brain regions involved in memory and emotion. Neurons there, in turn, send fibers to the fully conscious, decision-making frontal lobes, where yet other cells in the chain of communication feed back signals to the "lower" structures.

Many abusable substances, including cocaine and benzodiazepines (such as Valium) operate in this circuit. An effect common to several of them involves neurons that originate in the brain stem and connect to a nearby structure called the nucleus accumbens. They employ a chemical called dopamine, one of several dozen such "neurotransmitters" by which neurons communicate to cells they touch.

NALTREXONE TO ASSIST ABSTINENCE

Researchers in Philadelphia gave naltrexone, a drug that blocks opiate receptors, to 70 male alcoholics. Use of the drug lowered the rate of relapse.

In percent of people that showed no relapse*

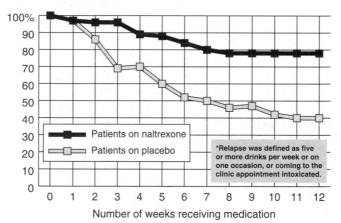

Number of weeks receiving medication

Source: *Washington Post National Weekly Edition*, April 25–May 1, 1994.

Alcohol, researchers now know, increases the amount or potency of dopamine released onto cells in the nucleus accumbens. Rats bred or trained to like alcohol show an increase in dopamine in the nucleus accumbens when they push the levers in their cages that give them a dose. The augmentation of this neurotransmitter appears to be essential—or at least very important—to the chemical reward and reinforcement that develops in alcoholics.

It is possible to affect dopamine-signaling neurons with drugs. The so-called neuroleptics, such as Thorazine and Haldol, used to treat hallucinations do just that. These medicines, however, have substantial side effects. Alcohol researchers looked for other entries to the neuronal circuit of alcohol dependency.

As it happens, neurons using opiate-like substances as their neurotransmitters exist both where the dopamine cells originate and where they send their signaling tentacles. The opiate cells modulate the activity of dopamine cells. The details of the interaction, however, are unknown.

Nevertheless, experiments in rats have found that stimulating the opiate receptors on dopamine cells with low doses of morphine makes rats drink more alcohol. Conversely, blocking the receptors with "opiate antagonist" drugs causes the animals to drink less.

NALTREXONE

Several years ago, Joseph R. Volpicelli and Charles P. O'Brien of the Philadelphia Veterans Affairs Medical Center applied these laboratory observations to alcoholic patients. They randomly assigned 70 men to receive either the opiate antagonist naltrexone or placebo for a 12-week period. Neither the doctors nor the patients knew which they were getting.

Men on naltrexone reported less craving for alcohol, and fewer days on which they drank. Though more patients on placebo were absolutely abstinent, significantly more of them relapsed to uncontrolled drinking than those on naltrexone. Furthermore, people on the opiate blocker said they experienced less of the usual high from alcohol.

A similar study was later done at Yale University School of Medicine, in New Haven, Conn. Naltrexone there also proved more effective than placebo in preventing relapse, reducing the number of drinking days, and decreasing the severity of alcohol-induced medical problems.

The Yale study had a surprise finding that underscored the psychological complexity of alcohol dependence and illustrated why it is unlikely a drug will ever be a "magic bullet" in the battle for sobriety.

In addition to taking either naltrexone or placebo, the people in the study were also assigned to counseling. Half got "coping skills" therapy, in which they were taught to analyze their drinking behavior, monitor their urges and rehearse strategies for resisting a desire to drink. The other half got "supportive" therapy, which consisted of more ordinary encouragement to stay abstinent and offered less psychological insight into the perils of relapse.

Those on naltrexone and supportive therapy did far better

than the people on naltrexone and coping skills therapy. By focusing so much on the pitfalls of abstinence, the coping skills therapy may have actually made backsliding a self-fulfilling prophecy, Stephanie S. O'Malley, the chief researcher, told a forum at the National Institute on Alcohol Abuse and Alcoholism (NIAAA).

"There may have been a problem of *anticipating* relapse in the discussion of relapse in the coping group," she says.

PROZAC

The complicated mix of conscious and subconscious forces that makes up addiction and abstinence was suggested by another study discussed at the NIAAA meeting. A small, previously reported experiment from Canada involving heavy drinkers who wanted to cut down, but not necessarily quit, drinking had shown that use of fluoxetine, the antidepressant marketed as Prozac, provided a modest but clear beneficial effect. Henry R. Kranzler, a psychiatrist at the University of Connecticut Health Center, hypothesized this effect might be enhanced by psychotherapy.

He ran a study in which heavy drinkers were divided into two groups, one getting fluoxetine, the other placebo, but all getting psychotherapy. At the end of three months, both groups had reduced their drinking the same amount.

Kranzler speculated that fluoxetine's effect may have been transient, or perhaps simply too weak to be detected in the presence of a more potent treatment, namely psychotherapy. At the same time, however, a subgroup of drinkers who met the diagnosis for depression did seem to do better on fluoxetine than on placebo, he said.

This suggests that abusers of alcohol are a heterogeneous population, and no single treatment strategy is likely to work for them all.

| "Buddhism deepened my belief in the 12-Step process."

BUDDHISM CAN HELP ALCOHOLICS STAY SOBER

Pat Patton

In the following viewpoint, Pat Patton argues that the tenets of Buddhism are consistent with the twelve steps of Alcoholics Anonymous and other twelve-step recovery programs. Patton writes that her knowledge of and belief in Buddhism has helped her to understand and follow the twelve steps in order to remain sober and experience a spiritual awakening. Patton is a psychotherapist in private practice in Boulder and Westminster, Colorado.

As you read, consider the following questions:
1. What is "the magic of 12-Step recovery," in Patton's opinion?
2. How does the author describe the teaching of "basic goodness"?
3. What does Patton say she had to "let go" of as part of her recovery process?

From Pat Patton, "Twelve Steps, God Optional," *Shambhala Sun*, May 1995 (adapted from the original article in the Naropa Institute's *Journal of Contemplative Psychology*, 1995). Reprinted by permission of the author.

Since God, for many nontheists, is the major obstacle to acceptance of the 12-Step recovery process from addiction, I want to give evidence here of the inspirational intention of the God aspect of 12-Step work, an intent shared by all spiritual paths, theistic and nontheistic.

The 12-Step program is not a religion. It is a spiritual path, with three indispensable spiritual principles which represent the "HOW" (how it works) of the program: Honesty, Open-mindedness, and Willingness.

The understanding of a higher power is up to the addict. Some call it "the group" or "the program," and most understand God, or Higher Power, as simply whatever force keeps them sober. Gerald May in his book *Addiction and Grace,* quotes Paul Tillich, who said that whatever we are ultimately concerned with is God for us.

During the early days and years of sobriety, staying sober is the addict's ultimate concern. This ultimate focus becomes God for the addict, by whatever name or image given, to enable the addict to achieve sobriety. For many 12-Step members this focus is easily translated into the traditional belief in God. Yet there are people with successful recoveries who do *not* believe in such a being.

I was not a traditional believer in God at the beginning of my recovery, nor am I now. However I saw ample evidence of a responsive creative force, answering cries for help, that was beyond the ordinary. Trusting this force opened my eyes to countless "miracles" of synchronicity, coincidence, and extraordinary human transformations.

A Necessary Part of Recovery

Julia Cameron says in *The Artist's Way,* "Whether we conceive of an inner god force or an other, outer God, doesn't matter. Relying on that force does." This force, or God or Self or group, that extends beyond the individual to a larger reality, which is obtained by a definite, conscious process, is a necessary part of 12-Step recovery.

The concept of a higher power allows the addict to reach out for help in order to let go of entrenched belief systems rooted in self-centeredness. Asking for help, letting go of one's control, one's ego, is difficult enough without the added burden of addiction. For most, the concept of a higher power affords the inspiration to move forward.

The magic of 12-Step recovery—and I think the major reason for its recognized success in comparison to other treatment forms—is the surrender to a higher intelligence. Wisdom traditions throughout history refer to this higher power both internally and externally, regardless of the name, over and over again. So yes, I believe in a higher power. You might say I think of God as a verb, and I see that active concept moving the mind, the body, and the spirit away from addiction.

12 STEPS FOR BUDDHISTS

A nontheistic translation of the 12 Steps of Alcoholics Anonymous

1. Having examined our body, speech and mind through the practice of meditation, we realized that our lives had become unworkable due to excessive use of alcohol.

2. Realized through the discipline and practice of communication with others and the realization of our own basic goodness that we could rediscover our brilliant sanity.

3. Through refuge in and devotion to the Three Jewels [Buddha, Dharma, Sangha], made a decision to cultivate and practice mindfulness and egolessness regarding alcohol in our lives.

4. Exercised exertion and fearlessness in our honest assessment of ourselves through meditation, contemplation and the study of the teachings.

5. Engaged with our world, ourselves and another person openly and straightforwardly concerning our use of alcohol and how it has affected our lives.

6. Were entirely willing to surrender to our own basic goodness.

7. Became willing to work on ourselves.

8. Through working further with our minds, recognized the past, present and future potential for causing pain to others inherent in our misuse of alcohol.

9. Made a firm commitment to work with others, exchange self with others.

10. Exercised further effort and fearlessness in the exploration of our own minds through a yet more thorough, ongoing practice of the dharma, driving all blames into one.

11. Took every opportunity offered by our fortunate births to actively practice and live in the dharma with devotion, love and respect for the Three Jewels and our own sacred world.

12. Having gained unshakeable insight as a result of this process, we committed ourselves in a spirit of nonreturning generosity to work with others.

The Buddhist Alcohol Study Group, *Shambhala Sun*, May 1995.

I do question the absolutism of the program. In truth, to say anything against the 12-Step process scares me and smacks of betrayal. But it is not perfect. Buddhism created a more spacious view for me, and it complemented my ongoing recovery. I want to share with you how Buddhism deepened my belief in the 12-Step process.

ENCOUNTERING SUFFERING

Step 1: We admitted we were powerless over our addiction and our lives had become unmanageable.

Perhaps the most fundamental of Buddhist teachings is the Four Noble Truths, which the Buddha formulated as a summary of his realization. When I contemplate the First Noble Truth, which speaks to the nature of suffering in life, my appreciation of Step 1 is deepened. When I remember my powerlessness over alcohol, I am reminded of my suffering; in fact, Step 1 was originally written, "We knew we were whipped." That is suffering, certainly.

Meditation practice led me to a deeper encounter with my suffering, beyond just the pain resulting from alcohol abuse. One day on my cushion, after weeks of meditation, I felt emotional pain more acutely than ever before. It had no story line. It was just pain. For once I did not give it excuses for being, such as my mother's death or failed relationships or slights to my ego. I just felt it.

I am sure I had known such pain before, but meditation practice allowed me to experience its depths and accept it as a condition of existence. I had always pushed pain away, first with my religion, then with anesthetization through alcohol.

Abstinence does not produce a manageable life. Buddhism influenced my interpretation of "unmanageability" in terms of *samsara*, the struggle to survive through habitual patterns. Just by assuming the posture of meditation, by taking my seat on the spot, I get a sense that my life is workable. Instead of focusing on problems, which revolve around "me," "ego," I can let go of habitual preoccupations such as denial, rationalization, justification and, most important, self-aggression. I may recognize *feelings* of powerlessness, but I am not powerless.

When I had been sober about six months, I remember talking on the phone one morning, holding a cup of coffee and catching sight of a pen rolling off a table behind my back. I caught it in midair, effortlessly. I cried happy tears over that. Why? Because during my addiction, my sense perceptions were so drugged that I could not have done that. With that simple feat of coordination, I felt a keen sense of dignity and oneness with the universe.

Basic Goodness

Step 2: We came to believe that a power greater than ourselves could restore us to sanity.

Incomprehensible in my early days of Buddhist studies was the fundamental teaching of "basic goodness." This teaching proclaims that all beings possess an intrinsic and undeniable wakefulness, called Buddha-nature. Addiction is a distancing journey away from our true self, our basic goodness. Coming home to that is the ultimate path—again and again.

Coming from "basic badness" and a spiritual background infused with original sin, I find that embracing the concept of my own basic goodness has become a power force from within, rather than from "out there." To me, it is the God within. To view my basic, true nature as one of peace and gentleness restores my sanity, and it eases my paranoia by allowing me to see that quality more clearly in others.

Letting Go of Ego

Step 3: We made a decision to turn our will and our lives over to the care of God as we understand him.

"Letting go" was a term frequently expressed during my early exposure to Buddhism. Its similarity to "Let God" provided my first comparison to 12-Step philosophy.

Learning to let go is vital to recovery. And you feel really good when you do, and really bad and obsessive when you do not. I learned many action steps in recovery for living my life better, but heard no tips on how to let go. Timidly, I would wonder, "Let go of what?"

The Buddhist answer was "Let go of ego." Buddhism taught me this lesson gently and with patience on the meditation cushion. For hours I watched my mind hold on to thoughts. Then thoughts would disappear. I saw the power of my ego, just as I had seen the power of alcohol, and I saw how by letting go of ego, I was able to let go of alcohol, as well as of other deeply ingrained habitual patterns.

Step 4: We made a searching and fearless moral inventory of ourselves.

With this step, I came to appreciate *maitri*, or kindness towards oneself. As explained by Osel Tendzin in *Buddha in the Palm of Your Hand*, "We have to accept negativity as part of our path. In order to do that we have to make friends with ourselves completely, by developing what is known as *maitri*, or loving kindness. Kindness to ourselves means kindness to whatever negativity arises and to whatever seems to be outside our discipline. We have to learn to relax and readmit chaos, which means having an open heart."

Step 4 includes some goodness along with the bad, but there is no acceptance of the bad. It is something to be rid of. Making friends with myself was the hardest friendship I have ever forged. My self-talk was merciless, and the experience of *maitri* has bubbled up slowly.

"Bringing in More Light"

Step 5: We admitted to God, to ourselves, and to another human being, the exact nature of our wrongs.

Through Buddhism, I learned the story of the great yogin Milarepa and his guru Marpa. Milarepa labored many years to relate to his past actions and the chaos he had created by using sorcery to wreak destruction. It was necessary for him to take full responsibility for the harm he had caused, before he could receive instructions that led to his liberation.

While the 12-Step process suggests a need to get rid of my wrongs, I now have space to own it all—the good, the bad, and the good intent gone awry. I have come to think of enlightenment as zen master Charlotte Joko Beck describes it—"bringing in more light." Like mushrooms, defects grow in the dark, and die in the light of exposure.

Step 6: We were entirely ready to have God remove all these defects of character.

I no longer expect to be permanently rid of my defects. Take patience, for example. Through practice I have increased this virtue, but impatience will come back. As I increase awareness of my numerous states of mind and behaviors, I am able to work more skillfully with them when they do arise. I no longer view them as setbacks to my recovery. My journey in this life is more focused on learning the art of being a better human being, rather than on being a perfect one.

Step 7: Humbly ask Him to remove our shortcomings.

Here, also, I seek my better self, my basic goodness. I think of shortcomings as the clouds that impede the view of my true nature. Humility, to me, means being teachable. I want to be more spacious, more open to the transformation of destructive behavior into positive behavior. That happens, too.

Making Amends

Step 8: We made a list of all persons we had harmed and became willing to make amends to them all.

Step 9: We made direct amends to such people whenever possible except when to do so would injure them or others.

Step 10: We continued to take personal inventory and when we were wrong promptly admitted it.

I know that during my active addiction I harmed a lot of people, but I hurt myself most of all. I have made amends to myself now, as well as to others. I have found I can ease my shame and guilt through developing *maitri*. My search for authenticity and my basic goodness lead me away from harming others, and to painful awareness when I do.

This deepening interpretation of these steps has helped me realize the possibility of egolessness and to realize that we humans are not unchangeable, but ever-changing and growing. My favorite of the mind training slogans is "Drive all blames into oneself." Beginning with the story of Adam and Eve, I have observed a world quick to blame others (even a snake!) for all discomfort.

This slogan demands that I come back inside myself and realize how my preoccupation with self allows me to sacrifice others. It demands an immediate search for how I am projecting my pain outward and results in a clearer vision of both self and other.

Another slogan is "Be grateful to everyone." Not only am I quicker to make amends, but I have come to know that the anxiety and frustration which emerge in relationships are my most direct route to self-awareness. I not only want to make amends; I am consistently grateful for the irritations.

A Spiritual Awakening

Step 11: We sought through prayer and meditation to improve our conscious contact with God as we understood Him, praying only for knowledge of His will for us and the power to carry that out.

Step 12: Having had a spiritual awakening as a result of these steps, we tried to carry this message to others and to practice these principles in all our affairs.

A "spiritual awakening" previously had a religious connotation to me. Today I see it as a powerful glimpse of my basic goodness.

"Unconditional love" is a term heard frequently in meetings. And practiced. It is an uplifting view of others that I have never witnessed outside those 12-Step meeting rooms. I remember an NA meeting called "Moon Dog." It was held on Friday night, a night when the 200-plus people in this group traditionally liked to "howl." The meeting was mixed: whites, blacks, gays, straights, rich, poor, homeless, ordinary, and famous. At the end of the meeting, all 200 voices quietly recited, "God grant me the serenity to accept the things I cannot change, the courage to change the things I can and the wisdom to know the difference." And then came a deafening final roar: "Keep coming back!"

Was this sense of joy and renewal just some sort of emotional release? Maybe in part. But today I believe that associating with people from vastly different social and economic strata, without judgment, affords a release from the life-deadening force of conditioned response. In those moments of intense awareness of the present, with gratitude for lives almost lost, we were given a glimpse of basic goodness in others and ourselves that ordinary associations do not afford. The "Moon Dog" meeting never failed to provide a "spiritual awakening."

Over the years I have watched hundreds of people pass through the doors of 12-Step meetings. Many come back— most do not. The ones who do and who practice the 12 Steps wake up spiritually. This awakening is evidenced by the changes made in hopeless lives. These people realize their own dignity. They realize they have the strength to practice a set of disciplines. As compassion is felt within, there is a strong desire to share it with others. For many, this is the first time they think beyond self.

PERIODICAL BIBLIOGRAPHY

The following articles have been selected to supplement the
diverse views presented in this chapter. Addresses are provided
for periodicals not indexed in the *Readers' Guide to Periodical Literature*, the *Alternative Press Index*, the *Social Sciences Index*, or the *Index to
Legal Periodicals and Books*.

Marianne Apostolides   "How to Quit the Holistic Way," *Psychology Today*, September/October 1996.

Geoffrey Cowley et al.   "A New Assault on Addiction," *Newsweek*, January 30, 1995.

Andrew Delbanco and Thomas Delbanco   "A.A. at the Crossroads," *New Yorker*, March 20, 1995.

Steve Hamilton   "Getting with the Program," *Crossroads*, April 1993.

Mark Gauvreau Judge   "Alcoholism: Character or Genetics?" *Insight*, March 3, 1997. Available from 3600 New York Ave. NE, Washington, DC 20002.

Mark Gauvreau Judge   "Recovery's Next Step," *Common Boundary*, January/February 1994.

Harry C. Kiely   "The Demon of Addiction," *Sojourners*, May/June 1996.

Audrey Kishline   "A Toast to Moderation," *Psychology Today*, January/February 1996.

Susan Kissir   "Treat Alcoholism with Nutrition," *Natural Health*, January/February 1993. Available from PO Box 7440, Red Oak, IA 51591-0440.

Alan Marlatt   "Top Ten Reasons Why Alcoholism Is an Addiciton but Not a Disease," *Professional Counselor*, October 1996.

Jill Neimark et al.   "Back from the Drink," *Psychology Today*, September/October 1994.

Stanton Peele   "Recovering from an All-or-Nothing Approach to Alcohol," *Psychology Today*, September/October 1996.

Jill Sell   "Alcoholism: Genetics or the Environment?" *Priorities*, vol. 7, no. 1, 1995. Available from the American Council on Science and Health, 1995 Broadway, 2nd Fl., New York, NY 10023-5860.

Michele Turk   "For Problem Drinkers, a Moderate Proposal," *BusinessWeek*, October 23, 1995.

CHAPTER

WHAT MEASURES SHOULD BE TAKEN TO REDUCE ALCOHOL-RELATED PROBLEMS?

CHAPTER PREFACE

Policy makers and public health experts promote various measures designed to reduce alcohol-related problems such as drunk driving and alcoholism. These measures are often aimed at teenagers and young adults, who are considered particularly at risk for such problems due to their inexperience with alcohol and their susceptibility to peer pressure. While such efforts are undertaken in the public arena, however, parents face the more personal task of deciding how to teach their children about alcohol.

Some parents believe that teens—particularly those in their late teens and those preparing to go away to college—should be allowed to drink at home. These parents contend that their teenage children will likely be exposed to alcohol before they reach the legal drinking age of twenty-one. In order to prepare teenagers for the inevitable encounters with alcohol, these parents argue, parents should teach their children how to drink responsibly and moderately within the safety of their own home. According to Elizabeth Whelan, who is president of the American Council on Science and Health and the mother of a college-age daughter, "In parts of the Western world, moderate drinking by teenagers and even children under their parents' supervision is a given. . . . Kids learn to regard moderate drinking as an enjoyable family activity rather than as something they have to sneak away to do. Banning drinking by young people makes it a badge of adulthood—a tantalizing forbidden fruit."

Others reject the contention that allowing teenagers to drink at home will ensure their safety. For example, Cynthia S. Roark, president of the San Diego County chapter of Mothers Against Drunk Driving, states, "When parents 'bargain' with youth—i.e., allow them to drink at home as long as they promise not to drink and drive—the youth are more likely to drive after drinking or be in a vehicle driven by someone who has been drinking." In order to help prevent drunk driving and other alcohol-related problems among teenagers, Roark and others insist, parents must consistently send the message that underage drinking is unacceptable under any circumstances.

Ultimately, parents must choose what they feel is the most appropriate course of action for informing their own children about the potential hazards of alcohol. Meanwhile, policy makers will continue to devise societal measures, such as those discussed in the following chapter, to combat alcohol-related problems among young people.

| "The weight of the evidence to date shows that . . . when alcohol taxes go up, heavy drinking, drunk driving, cirrhosis, and traffic fatalities fall."

RAISING ALCOHOL TAXES COULD REDUCE ALCOHOL-RELATED PROBLEMS

Donald S. Kenkel

Some economists and policy makers advocate increased taxes on alcohol (sometimes referred to as sin taxes) as a means of deterring people from abusing alcohol. In the following viewpoint, Donald S. Kenkel argues that research has demonstrated that higher alcohol taxes result in lower rates of alcohol-related problems such as drunk driving and cirrhosis of the liver. Although he concedes that alcohol taxes impose burdens on those who drink responsibly and moderately, Kenkel maintains that such taxes have the potential to reduce the economic and social costs of alcohol abuse. Kenkel is an associate professor in the Department of Consumer Economics and Housing at Cornell University in Ithaca, New York.

As you read, consider the following questions:

1. What would be the consequences of a 10 percent increase in alcohol prices, according to Kenkel's estimate?
2. How do the health benefits of moderate drinking compare to the health costs of heavy drinking, in the author's opinion?
3. What are the "external costs" of alcohol abuse, as described by Kenkel?

Excerpted from Donald S. Kenkel, "Taxing Alcohol to Improve Public Health," *Cornell Consumer Close-Ups*, 1995-96:2. Reprinted by permission of the author. (Notes/references in the original have been omitted here.)

The abuse of alcohol continues to be a significant public health problem. In 1988 26,000 people died of cirrhosis of the liver, making it the ninth leading cause of death in the U.S. Alcohol is involved in almost half of all fatal car crashes, and is believed to be a factor in many other accidents, homicides, and suicides, as well as contributing to serious illnesses other than cirrhosis. All told, it has been estimated that over 100,000 deaths a year are attributable to alcohol.

Except during Prohibition, the taxation of alcohol has also been an enduring part of U.S. fiscal policy. Alexander Hamilton, the first secretary of the Treasury, persuaded Congress to tax whiskey to help pay off war debts. The Philadelphia College of Physicians supported Hamilton's proposal, based on their combined professional opinion that "a great proportion of the most obstinate, painful, and mortal disorders which affect the human body are produced by distilled spirits." One result of this early effort to tax alcohol was the Whiskey Rebellion of 1794. Recent alcohol tax increases have been less dramatic, but have been motivated by a similar combination of fiscal and health concerns. . . .

TAXES AND ALCOHOL ABUSE

Economists have accumulated a body of evidence suggesting that higher alcohol taxes reduce drinking, even heavy and abusive drinking. Differences in the alcohol beverage taxes over time and across the states have provided a series of "natural experiments" shedding light on the tax-consumption relationship. The ideal would be to compare alcohol consumption by individuals who face different tax rates but who are otherwise identical. The data provided by natural policy experiments do not provide this ideal, so it is necessary to use econometric models that control statistically for the other factors that influence drinking. To the extent the econometric methods are appropriate, the remaining differences in drinking can be attributed to differences in taxes.

Econometric studies have found systematic relationships between alcohol taxes and a variety of alcohol-related outcome measures, including cirrhosis rates, traffic fatality rates, alcoholic beverage purchases, and self-reported heavy drinking and drunk driving. Taken together, these studies make a convincing case that increasing alcohol taxes can be an effective tool to reduce heavy drinking. . . .

My research adds to this literature, generally confirming earlier results. Using data from the 1985 Health Interview Survey, I estimated that a tax increase that raises alcohol prices by 10 percent leads to somewhere between a 5 to 10 percent decrease in heavy drinking and drunk driving. I also estimated that stricter drunk driving laws could deter drunk driving, with one policy scenario leading to a 20 percent reduction in drunk driving.

It is important to recognize what the econometric results mean. The results do not mean that every heavy drinker sobers up in response to higher prices. There are surely some individuals who fit the stereotype of the problem drinker who will continue to abuse alcohol despite almost any cost, monetary or otherwise. In fact, my results and the results of another study by Willard Manning, Linda Blumberg and Lawrence Moulton suggest a subset of the heaviest drinkers are unresponsive to price. The econometric results indicate, however, that this stereotype does not fit all heavy drinkers. The weight of the evidence to date shows that enough drinkers respond to price so that when alcohol taxes go up, heavy drinking, drunk driving, cirrhosis, and traffic fatalities fall.

WHAT ABOUT MODERATE DRINKING?

The majority of drinkers consume alcohol at moderate levels unlikely to result in serious health or safety consequences. Clearly, taxing alcohol to prevent the adverse consequences of heavy drinking imposes a burden on these responsible drinkers. It is probably impossible to design a tax structure that could tax heavy drinking and exempt moderate drinking. Practically speaking, an unavoidable limitation of alcohol taxation is that it is a blunt policy tool.

In addition to the financial burden taxes place on moderate drinkers, there is the possibility their health could suffer even as taxes improve the health of alcohol abusers. Some medical evidence suggests that moderate drinking (no more than two to three drinks per day) may help protect against cardiovascular disease. The econometric evidence indicates that moderate drinkers are likely to reduce their consumption in response to a price increase. This raises the possibility that alcohol taxes will move some moderate drinkers [toward] a higher mortality rate. However, the health benefits of moderate drinking appear to be quite modest compared to the health costs of heavy drinking.

BALANCING PRIVATE AND PUBLIC INTERESTS

Even taking into account the possible beneficial effects of moderate drinking, it is likely that the net effect of increasing alcohol taxes would be an improvement in public health. Yet this does not necessarily mean that higher alcohol taxes are a desirable public policy.

Taxing alcohol to improve health could be justified on paternalistic grounds. One interpretation is that the government is taxing heavy drinkers "for their own good." By a similar rationale, the government should be taxing junk food and subsidizing bran cereal, again for our "own good." Many people support limited policies along these lines, including cigarette taxation. But many people would agree that government health policies towards private health decisions could easily become too intrusive. This suggests the need for a systematic approach to balancing private and public interests in health.

ALCOHOL COSTS EXCEED TAX REVENUES

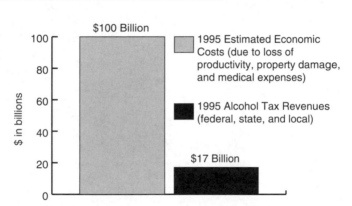

Center for Science in the Public Interest, *State Alcohol Taxes & Health: A Citizen's Action Guide*, 1996.

The "optimal corrective taxation" approach adopted by economists is based not on paternalism but on the distinction between private and external costs. When people abuse alcohol, they impose costs on others. The most dramatic external costs are the thousands of nondrinkers killed by drunk drivers each year. Additional external costs stem from the adverse health effects of heavy drinking, which create medical and other costs that are only partly borne by the drinker. The individual drinker who bases his or her consumption decisions only on private costs fails to take into account these external costs. If applied appropriately, the optimal tax "internalizes" the external costs, so that individual drinkers base their choices on the full costs associated with their actions.

Several studies have combined this approach with econometric evidence to develop estimates of the optimal tax on alcohol. Given the uncertainties and limitations of these studies, this line of research has not yielded an estimate of the exactly correct rate. Still, several general conclusions have emerged.

First, . . . the studies indicate that the substantial external costs associated with heavy drinking warrant higher taxes, even taking into account the burden taxation places on moderate drinkers. But second, alcohol taxation is a blunt policy tool to reduce the problems associated with alcohol abuse. I estimate that the optimal tax rate would be much lower (although still above today's levels) if punishment for drunk driving were more certain and severe. Since stiffer deterrence policies are also costly, the best mix of taxation, other alcohol control policies, and deterrence remains an open and important policy question.

| "Raising taxes on alcohol would target the wrong population and do little to remedy the problem."

RAISING ALCOHOL TAXES WOULD NOT REDUCE ALCOHOL-RELATED PROBLEMS

Dwight B. Heath

In the following viewpoint, Dwight B. Heath argues against the theory that raising alcohol taxes would help to combat the problems associated with alcohol abuse. According to Heath, higher taxes on alcohol would not lead to a decrease in alcohol use or drunk driving by heavy drinkers. Furthermore, if alcohol taxes were increased, responsible drinkers would cut down on alcohol and would thereby be denied the health benefits associated with moderate drinking. Heath is a professor of anthropology at Brown University in Providence, Rhode Island, and a scientific adviser to the American Council on Science and Health, a consumer education organization that studies issues related to food, chemicals, and human health.

As you read, consider the following questions:

1. What are the false premises underlying the proposal to raise alcohol taxes, according to Heath?
2. How do Scandinavian countries combat drunk driving, according to the author?

From Dwight B. Heath, "Alcohol Tax Hike Will Not Affect Mortality," *Jamestown* (N.Y.) *Sunday Post-Journal*, June 18, 1995. Reprinted by permission of the author.

W e have all heard about the inevitability of death and taxes. Now comes an interesting new theory: that you can reduce the one—mortality—by increasing the other.

This notion is offered in an exchange in the *New England Journal of Medicine*, a leading medical journal.

In 1995, the *Journal* published a careful study demonstrating that alcohol-related traffic fatalities were much more likely to occur among drivers with previous arrests for driving while intoxicated than among those who were not repeat offenders. In other words, it's the problem drinkers, not the rest of us, who are the primary source of alcohol-related injury and death on the road.

How to stop the carnage? One physician, in a letter to the editors, suggests that the way to reduce the alcohol-related mayhem is to raise taxes on alcoholic beverages. The physician proposing this measure referred to his remedy as a "sin tax."

FALSE PREMISES

The assumptions underlying the proposal are that:
- Taxing all drinkers will prevent problem drinkers from causing mayhem on the roads.
- Other, more targeted and effective means to prevent the carnage from drunk drivers are not available.
- No health benefits would be lost by taxing alcohol.

All these premises are false.

We know from the carefully monitored experiences of Finland and Sweden that moderate drinkers (those who have no more than two drinks a day) cut back when taxes escalate, but heavy drinkers (five or more drinks per occasion) do not. Since more than half of all those arrested for DWI have been found to be alcoholics, it should be obvious raising taxes on alcohol would target the wrong population and do little to remedy the problem.

We also know the increasingly popular custom of using a designated driver keeps many social drinkers from taking the risk of driving while under the influence. Heavy drinkers, on the other hand, tend to resist that approach and remain a risk to themselves and to others.

The Scandinavian countries use mandatory prison sentences for the first offense (sometimes served over successive weekends so it doesn't interfere with employment), automatic revocation of licenses, and similar penalties aimed at serious offenders.

A further tax on alcoholic beverages—already among the most heavily taxed and regulated commodities in most jurisdictions—would probably take food out of the family budgets of heavy drinkers, while doing little to diminish either heavy drinking or drunken driving among those for whom these behaviors are habitual.

Costs Do Not Exceed Existing Tax Rate

Recently, economists have entered the alcohol policy arena by pointing out that consumption, and also abuse, may be reduced through price increases induced by taxation. . . . The notion that abuse can be curbed by taxation has led to a call for increased taxes on alcohol. However, the economic justification for a tax increase is that it meet the social cost-efficiency criterion—that is, the marginal external cost of alcohol abuse should exceed the existing marginal tax rate. . . .

The evidence . . . indicates that the net external costs of alcohol do not exceed the current level of taxation. Much like the case for the taxation of tobacco, the rationale for a tax increase on alcohol does not pass the social-cost test when all costs, including those imposed on moderate drinkers, are juxtaposed against the current levels of taxation.

Dale M. Heien, *Cato Journal*, Fall/Winter 1995/96.

Finally, it makes no sense to adopt a policy that would deny moderate drinkers the cardiovascular health benefits that have been well-established in recent years for sensible drinking. Yet, since moderate drinkers are the ones who reduce alcohol intake in the face of increased taxes, this is what would happen.

Drinking Is Not the Problem

It's important to remember it's not drinking, per se, that's the problem; it's the irresponsible behavior of the problem drinker.

Irresponsible people who put themselves and others at risk should be punished. But those who drink responsibly, causing no harm to themselves or others—that is, fully 90 percent of all Americans who choose to drink—should be allowed to enjoy the sociability, relaxation and health benefits of moderate drinking without being penalized for somebody else's problem.

It would be wise for policy makers to remember that with respect to public health—as well as other social policy—symbolic action like raising taxes on alcohol is not the answer. Substantive targeting of the problem with an effective solution is.

"Passage of age-21 laws in many states has significantly reduced youth drinking, traffic crash involvement, and other health problems."

MINIMUM DRINKING-AGE LAWS SHOULD BE STRONGLY ENFORCED

Alexander C. Wagenaar and Mark Wolfson

In the following viewpoint, Alexander C. Wagenaar and Mark Wolfson maintain that despite the existence of minimum-age drinking laws, an unacceptable number of young people under twenty-one continue to obtain and consume alcoholic beverages. The authors contend that in order to reduce underage drinking, minimum-age drinking laws must be enforced more strongly. Efforts should be directed at penalizing commercial outlets and other sources that provide alcohol to minors, the authors argue. Wagenaar and Wolfson are associate professors of epidemiology at the University of Minnesota School of Public Health in Minneapolis.

As you read, consider the following questions:

1. In the study by D.F. Preusser and A.F. Williams, cited by the authors, what percentage of subjects were able to purchase beer in each of the three regions studied?
2. How frequently does underage drinking result in an arrest, according to Wagenaar and Wolfson? How frequently does it result in a penalty against an alcohol outlet?
3. In the authors' opinion, what enforcement mechanism should be used to deter commercial outlets from selling alcohol to minors?

Excerpted from Alexander C. Wagenaar and Mark Wolfson, "Enforcing the Legal Minimum Drinking Age in the United States," *Journal of Public Health Policy*, vol. 15, no. 1, Spring 1994. (Notes/references in the original have been omitted here.) Reprinted with permission.

Most American youth consume beverage alcohol, and the prevalence of use increases rapidly during adolescence. Approximately 6% of 10–11-year-olds are current (in the last month) users of alcohol; the rate increases to about 25% by ages 12–14, and to 55% by ages 15–17. Ninety-two percent of high school seniors report consuming alcohol at some point in their lives, and 64% report being current drinkers. Moreover, 35% report becoming intoxicated regularly (5+ drinks per occasion). Junior and senior high school–age youth drink an estimated 31.2 million gallons of wine coolers annually (35% of all wine coolers sold), and 1.1 billion cans of beer annually (2% of all beer sold). As a result of high rates of drinking, youth experience high rates of health and social problems associated with alcohol. Motor vehicle crashes are the leading cause of death for teenagers, with one-third to one-half involving alcohol. Other leading causes of death and long-term disability for youth, such as suicide, homicide, assault, drowning, and recreational injury, involve alcohol in substantial proportion. Although exact quantification of the health burden of underage alcohol consumption is difficult, underage alcohol use results in substantial premature deaths, disability, preventable hospitalizations, fiscal costs, and human suffering. As a result, extensive effort is expended to prevent youth drinking and its damaging sequelae.

One policy designed to reduce youth drinking and the traffic crashes and other problems that are associated with drinking is the minimum legal drinking age of 21. Passage of age-21 laws in many states has significantly reduced youth drinking, traffic crash involvement, and other health problems. . . . Age-21 laws have produced 10–15% declines in youth drinking and youth crash involvement. However, little is known about enforcement of the laws.

ALCOHOL IS EASILY OBTAINED

Several studies have documented the ease with which those under 21 can purchase alcoholic beverages despite laws prohibiting such sales. D.F. Preusser and A.F. Williams assessed how easy it was for 18–20-year-old males to purchase beer at off-premise retail outlets (e.g. liquor stores, convenience stores). Underage males successfully purchased packaged beer in 97% of attempts in Washington, D.C., 80% in Westchester County, New York, and 44% in Albany/Schenectady Counties, New York. J.A. McKnight briefly reported a similar study finding that underage youth were refused alcohol sales in only one-third of 100 establishments tested at eight sites around the United States. J.L. Forster and associates used 21-year-old female college students who were rated by a panel of judges to be age 17 to 19. Buyers made three separate purchase attempts at 112 liquor stores in 15 small communities in northern Minnesota. Buyers were able to purchase alcohol in 47% of the 336 attempts. The Minnesota research team significantly expanded the study, with analyses of 1800 purchase attempts at both on-premise outlets (e.g. bars, restaurants) and off-premise outlets (e.g. liquor stores, convenience stores) in 24 cities throughout Minnesota and Wisconsin. Results indicated that 47% of the outlets sold alcohol with no request for age identification. Finally, T. Radecki reported a successful buy rate of 52% in 53 cities throughout the U.S., using youth age 18–20 and a youthful 21-year-old as buyers.

Mike Keefe/*Denver Post*. Reprinted by permission of the artist.

Other studies have also documented the ease of youth access to alcohol despite the legal drinking age of 21. A.L. Wagenaar and associates studied patterns of acquisition of alcoholic beverages by underage youth using focus group methods with a sample of midwestern youth. Results showed that the initial alcohol used by those in their early teens is obtained from parents' stocks or from older siblings and friends. By the mid-teens, parties at which alcohol (usually beer) is readily available become the major source. In the mid- to late-teens, youth purchase alcohol from commercial alcohol outlets, despite the legal age of 21. Factors reported by youth to increase the rate of successful alcohol purchases include female buyer, male seller, young seller, and convenience store outlet.

The Office of the Inspector General of the Department of Human Services in 1991 released a series of reports on the minimum drinking age and youth drinking. Based on a survey of 956 students nationwide, two-thirds of 7th to 12th grade students in the U.S. who drink alcohol reportedly purchase their own alcoholic beverages. Methods used to purchase alcohol reported by underage students include using false identification, buying from stores that are known for selling to underage youth, and seeking young clerks.

AGE-21 LAW IS INADEQUATELY ENFORCED

The extant literature shows that most persons under the age of 21 are able to obtain alcohol, suggesting that this law is not rigorously enforced. . . .

Enforcement actions are minuscule compared to the frequency of underage drinking. Only two of every thousand occasions of illegal drinking by youth under 21 result in an arrest, and only five of every 100,000 youth drinking occasions result in an administrative action against an alcohol outlet.

We offer several recommendations. First, we must understand the manifest goal of drinking-age enforcement—to reduce the accessibility of alcohol to youth, with a consequent reduction in youth drinking and alcohol-related injuries and other problems. The mechanism by which enforcement will help achieve that end is via an increase in the deterrent effect of laws prohibiting sales or provision of alcohol to youth and prohibiting possession and consumption by youth. Despite relatively low levels of enforcement compared to number of offenses, tens of thousands of minors are arrested each year for possession or consumption of alcohol. In stark contrast, very few alcohol outlets that sell to minors or adults providing alcohol to minors are cited. Given: (1) there are over 18 million 16–20-year-olds in the U.S., most of whom use alcohol, (2) the frequency of youth drinking occasions, and (3) resource limits and other barriers to increasing arrest rates of minors in possession of alcohol, it may be difficult to rely on attempts to substantially increase the youth arrest rate to a level high enough to significantly deter youth drinking. On the other hand, there is a much smaller number of alcohol outlets that are a major source of alcohol for youth. With modest additional resources, sources of alcohol could be effectively targeted, significantly increasing deterrence of selling to minors. Moreover, an effective and efficient administrative mechanism to implement quick penalties on violators is available. Experience in drunk-driving control has demonstrated the effectiveness of administrative license suspension as a fast, efficient enforcement mechanism that is successful in deterring proscribed behavior. A promising avenue for enforcement of the drinking age is administrative suspension of licenses to sell alcoholic beverages. An increase in Alcohol Beverage Control enforcement actions can also easily be self-supporting, with fines generating revenues to cover the increased cost of policing. In addition to commercial sellers of alcohol, adults are the other main supplier of alcohol to underage youth, and enforcement efforts should also involve increased attention to those furnishing alcohol to underage youth. Focusing enforcement efforts on these two key pipelines for alcohol available to youth is likely to be much more efficient and effective than attempting to identify and arrest millions of underage drinkers.

MORE PERSONNEL AND DATA COLLECTION ARE NEEDED

Larger numbers of Alcohol Beverage Control enforcement personnel are urgently needed. Most states have only a few officers for thousands of alcohol outlets across an entire state. Many states are currently reducing even these minimal levels of enforcement staff. Increased assistance from state Alcohol Beverage Control agents would facilitate local police and sheriff departments' attention to alcohol control enforcement. In addition, one officer in each local enforcement agency should be designated as the alcohol control officer. Depending on the size of the department, part or all of that officer's salary could be covered with a program of returning a portion of state Alcohol Beverage Control fines to the locality which initiated the enforcement action.

Local law enforcement officers need multiple means of identifying outlets that sell to or serve minors. Regular sting operations, where an underage person enters establishments to purchase alcohol, appear easy to implement and may serve as an effective deterrent. In addition, for all police incidents involving those under age 21, officers should note whether alcohol was involved, and if so, attempt to identify and record the source of the alcohol consumed. Such data on source of alcohol for youth involved in police incidents should be provided to the officer designated for alcohol control enforcement, so that patterns of alcohol incidents can be reviewed to identify specific alcohol outlets that may be major sources of alcohol for youth. In addition to sting operations and recording source of alcohol at police-attended incidents, citizens can be encouraged to report alcohol outlets observed or suspected of selling to minors. Such outlets can then be given additional enforcement attention.

Each of the recommendations presented above has potential for reducing the availability of alcohol to youth. It is important to note that the organizational and political environments of minimum drinking age enforcement may sometimes pose significant obstacles to the implementation of these recommendations. Law enforcement officers often perceive a lack of support from their communities and from their own agencies for increased efforts to enforce the minimum drinking age. Increasing the focus on commercial outlets is especially problematic, given the political power of alcohol merchants in many local communities. In the end, successful implementation of these recommendations will hinge on political will to take meaningful action on drinking age enforcement.

| "It is not obvious that learning to drink with moderation . . . automatically happens to a 21-year-old as distinguished from someone three years younger."

MINIMUM DRINKING-AGE LAWS ARE INEFFECTIVE

William F. Buckley Jr.

As of 1988, every state had raised its legal minimum drinking age from eighteen to twenty-one. In the following viewpoint, William F. Buckley Jr. argues that this measure is unlikely to have caused any decrease in drunk-driving deaths. Delaying the age at which young people start to drink does not automatically ensure that they will drink responsibly, Buckley maintains. Rather than forbidding those between eighteen and twenty-one to drink, he contends, society should teach them to drink responsibly and to not drive while under the influence of alcohol. Buckley is a well-known commentator and the editor-at-large of *National Review*, a biweekly conservative magazine.

As you read, consider the following questions:

1. How has fraternity life been affected by laws forbidding those under twenty-one from drinking, according to Buckley?
2. According to the student interviewed by Buckley, why is it easier to get marijuana than beer in Cambridge?

Taken from William F. Buckley Jr., On the Right column, "The Eighteen-Year-Old and His/Her Beer," as it appeared in *Conservative Chronicle*, May 5, 1993. Copyright ©1993. Reprinted by permission of Universal Press Syndicate.

In 1984 the federal government put pressure on the states to lift the legal drinking age from 18 to 21. The feds used financial inducements of various kinds to get their way on the subject, and popular pressure was generated by citing the awful incidence of motor vehicle deaths caused by young people who had been drinking.

The statistics are not readily at hand on what has been the reduction in auto deaths with drunken 18-year-olds at the wheel, but whatever the figures are, they should be balanced by the number of deaths caused by young people who are 21, or 22. We know intuitively that if society succeeds in universally postponing the age at which a young man (or woman) has his first beer from 18 to 21, it is simply unrealistic to suppose that there has been an exact correlative maturity, bringing on prudence and responsibility on the 21st birthday.

Yes, obviously people are older at 21 than at 18; but no, it is not obvious that learning to drink with moderation, and not to drive when one is drinking, automatically happens to a 21-year-old as distinguished from someone three years younger. What a society needs to confront is how to teach young people to drink moderately and not to drink when driving a car is in prospect.

Alcohol and College Life

In colleges, where approximately 40 percent of Americans spend their time between ages 18 and 21, the no-drinking rule has had many interesting effects, most of them unpredicted. For one thing, fraternity life has quite generally palled. If the rules are followed, and no beer is permitted, the kind of post-pubescent bonhomie associated with college life is artificially inhibited. Indeed, many fraternities simply ceased to exist.

The alternative, of course, is to go ahead and make beer available with variable concern for surreptitious care. I have visited 100 colleges in the past few years, and though my inquiries have been far less than systematic, no one will question the generality that in some colleges, beer is quite generally available to 18-year-olds; in others, the law is a brooding omnipresence and beer drinking has to be done, so to speak, in the closet.

Now this has an effect on local eateries that everywhere are an integral part of college life. Meeting after a long working evening at Joe's for a hamburger and a beer is not something done only in novels by F. Scott Fitzgerald (in whose work gin was likelier to be the sophomore's drink, and the speakeasy the equivalent of Joe's). Depending on the local police, the eateries are strict in demanding to see an identification card when a young person orders a beer, or permissive on the question. It is altogether routine for students to acquire fake I.D.s, and by no means unusual for everyone concerned—the restaurant owner, the police, the college authorities—to know about these fake I.D.s and to do nothing about them, as they are useful cover for the formality of obeying the law.

FUTILE EFFORTS

Remorseless drinking has long been as much a ritual of university life as football, final exams and fret parties. Almost every college graduate can spin at least a few tales about a boisterous night of carousing that culminated in slugging shots of tequila at sunrise or tossing drained kegs into the president's pool. . . . Periodic efforts to crack down on excessive alcohol consumption among young scholars have been largely futile. Enforcing strict rules on university turf seemed to push the parties off campus. Raising the legal drinking age from 18 to 21 in the 1980s merely triggered a boom in the business of creating fake ID cards.

Christine Gorman, *Time*, December 19, 1994.

But strange and unexpected things happen when laws that contradict mores are enacted. A Harvard student told me that it is far easier in Cambridge, Massachusetts, to order marijuana than beer, because, he explained, the bar that sells a beer to the minor and is detected in the act stands to lose his entire capital plant: his license to serve liquor, his bar, and his inventory. The marijuana dealer generally has a capital plant that constitutes the depth of his two pockets. He is booked, his weed is confiscated and perhaps a few hundred dollars he has accumulated, and back he goes on the street to resume selling illegal pot.

Just as it is everywhere accepted that Prohibition coached an entire generation of Americans into the frivolity of law-breaking (we exaggerate: Many Americans obeyed the law and gave up drink, but they were not the style setters), so is it with young collegians, who are going to drink their beer whatever the law says, and are simply inconvenienced on how to do so.

If our federal system had been given a longer opportunity to work things out, the problem of drunken driving by older teenagers could have been faced as exactly that—the problem not of letting 18-year-olds drink beer, but of keeping 18-year-olds away from the wheel of a car when they do drink beer.

Another federal experiment up on the rocks of reality. So what else is new?

"Only a comprehensive . . . effort utilizing all parts of the college community can be expected to have an effect on this long-standing and deeply entrenched problem."

COLLEGES SHOULD COMBAT ALCOHOL ABUSE AMONG STUDENTS

Henry Wechsler

In recent years, various studies have suggested that binge drinking (typically defined as drinking five or more drinks in a row) is prevalent among college students. In the following viewpoint, Henry Wechsler presents the results of one such study conducted by the Harvard School of Public Health. According to the study, the high incidence of binge drinking results in problems for the entire college community—including injuries, property damage, and sexual assault. Wechsler argues that in response to this problem, colleges should devise anti-abuse programs that involve faculty, students, and members of local communities. Wechsler is a lecturer in the Department of Health and Social Behavior at the Harvard School of Public Health.

As you read, consider the following questions:

1. What was the single strongest predictor of binge drinking in the study described by the author?
2. What problems does binge drinking cause for non-binge drinkers, according to Wechsler?
3. How should colleges change the expectations of applicants and incoming freshmen, in the author's opinion?

It is hardly surprising that college presidents rank alcohol abuse as the No. 1 problem on campus. Widely used despite its illegality for most undergraduates, alcohol contributes to almost half of all motor vehicle fatalities—the leading cause of death among young Americans—and is associated with unintentional injuries as well as unsafe sex, a growing threat with the spread of AIDS and other sexually transmitted diseases.

Results from a recent Harvard School of Public Health College Alcohol Study provide the first national picture in almost 50 years of just how widespread and harmful heavy episodic or "binge" drinking has become, not only for those students who abuse alcohol, but also for others in their immediate environment. The picture that emerges from this survey of over 17,000 students on 140 campuses nationwide is not a pretty one. . . .

THE STUDY

We selected a national representative sample of colleges from the American Council on Education's list of four-year colleges and universities accredited by the six regional bodies covering the United States. One hundred forty accredited four-year colleges—72 percent of those asked—participated in the study. Located in 40 states and the District of Columbia, these institutions represent a cross-section of American higher education: two-thirds are public, and one-third are private; approximately two-thirds are located in suburban/urban settings, and one-third in small towns/rural settings; 4 percent are women-only colleges, and 4 percent are historically black institutions.

Our 20-page survey asked students a variety of questions about their drinking behavior and explored problems they experienced as a result of their own and other students' drinking. . . .

A sample of 25,627 students received questionnaires, and 17,592 students responded—an overall response rate of 69 percent. . . .

In this study, binge drinking is defined as five or more drinks in a row one or more times during a two-week period for men, and four or more drinks in a row one or more times during a two-week period for women—a gender-specific modification to a national standard measure. Our research documents that it takes four drinks for women to run the same risk of various alcohol-related health and behavior problems as men do with five drinks. These problems include getting into arguments, getting injured, forgetting where they were or what they did, and engaging in unplanned or unprotected sex. A drink is defined as a 12-ounce can or bottle of beer, a four-ounce glass of wine, a

12-ounce bottle or can of wine cooler, or a shot of liquor taken straight or in a mixed drink.

While some students may say four or five drinks isn't much, this study demonstrates that, for many students, this benchmark is indicative of a heavy drinking lifestyle. The data show that students who drink in these or greater amounts differ from other students by the frequency and severity of their alcohol-related problems. In reality, many students in this study report drinking far more than this, often with the specific intention of getting drunk.

THE PREVALENCE OF BINGE DRINKING

Fully 84 percent of all students reported drinking during the school year. Nearly half (44 percent) of all students were binge drinkers, and 19 percent were frequent binge drinkers (had binged three or more times in the previous two weeks). Even these averages, however, conceal the extent of heavy drinking on high-binge campuses.

Binging rates varied dramatically from campus to campus. At colleges with the lowest binge drinking reported, the rate was 1 percent of the student population. At the highest, it was a staggering 70 percent. At nearly one-third of the schools, more than half of the responding students were binge drinkers. We classified these schools as high-binge colleges.

Binge drinkers put themselves at high risk for many alcohol-related problems. The numbers in Table 1 illustrate the strong positive relationship between the frequency of drinking and a variety of alcohol-related health, social, and academic problems. Nearly half of frequent binge drinkers (47 percent) had experienced five or more different problems since the beginning of their school year as a result of their own drinking. In contrast, 14 percent of binge drinkers and only 3 percent of students who drink but do not binge experienced five or more different drinking-related problems. . . .

BINGING AND FRATERNITIES AND SORORITIES

The single strongest predictor of binge drinking was found to be fraternity or sorority residence or membership. Sorority members were nearly twice as likely to be binge drinkers as other college women (62 percent versus 35 percent, respectively). Among women who lived in sorority houses, an astonishing 80 percent were binge drinkers. Similarly, fraternity members binged more than other male students (75 percent versus 45 percent, respectively), and 86 percent of fraternity

TABLE 1. PERCENTAGE OF COLLEGE DRINKERS REPORTING ALCOHOL-RELATED PROBLEMS

Problem Experienced in Connection with Alcohol Use	Non-binge Drinkers(%)	Bingers (%)	Frequent Bingers (%)
Had a hangover	30	75	90
Did something they regretted later	14	37	63
Missed a class	8	30	61
Forgot where they were or what they did	8	26	54
Got behind in school work	6	21	46
Argued with friends	8	22	42
Engaged in unplanned sexual activity	8	20	41
Had unprotected sex	4	10	22
Got hurt or injured	2	9	23
Damaged property	2	8	22
Got into trouble with campus/local police	1	4	11
Required treatment for alcohol overdose	<1	<1	1

Source: Henry Wechsler, *Change*, July/August 1996.

house residents binged.

This raises the question of whether Greek societies attract or create binge drinkers. Our data indicate that both dynamics are at work. Sixty percent of those who lived in fraternity houses had been binge drinkers in high school, and over three-fourths of fraternity residents who had not binged in high school became binge drinkers in college. Conversely, sororities do not seem so much to attract prior binge drinkers; one in three women who lived in sororities had binged in high school—only slightly higher than the proportion among other students. But three out of every four women who had not binged in high school became binge drinkers while living in sorority houses.

SECONDHAND BINGE EFFECTS

The most troubling findings of this study reveal the impact of binge drinking on students who do not binge—the "second-hand" binge effects. It is no longer possible to view binging as solely the bingers' problem: non-binging students are paying too steep a price. Table 2 illustrates the secondhand problems at low- and high-binge campuses.

Comparing the prevalence of problems experienced by students at low-binge to those at high-binge schools brings the issue into sharp focus. On campuses where more than half the students are binge drinkers, the vast majority of students (87 percent) who live on campus have experienced one or more problems as a result of others' binge drinking. Even at schools where binge drinking rates are below 35 percent of the student population, 62 percent of students who live on campus have been victims of secondhand binge effects.

TABLE 2. PERCENTAGE OF STUDENTS AT LOW-BINGE AND HIGH-BINGE INSTITUTIONS REPORTING SECONDHAND ALCOHOL-RELATED PROBLEMS

| | Campus | |
Problem Due to Others' Drinking	Low-Binge	High-Binge
Was insulted or humiliated	21	34
Experienced unwanted sexual advances (based on women's responses only)	15	26
Had a serious argument or quarrel	13	20
Was pushed, hit, or assaulted	7	13
Studying or sleep was interrupted	42	68
Had to "baby-sit" a drunken student	31	54
Personal property was damaged	6	15
Suffered sexual assault or "date rape"	2	2

Source: Henry Wechsler, *Change*, July/August 1996.

In 1949, *Drinking in College* [by Robert Straus and Seldon Bacon] viewed drinking by women to be such a minor problem that the researchers defined five different levels of quantity and frequency for men but only two for women. Today, while women are still less likely to be binge drinkers than men, the gender gap has closed, and the risks to women are even more pronounced.

When women abuse alcohol, they increase their risk of being victimized by unwanted or unprotected sex. Female students are also especially at risk for serious secondhand binge effects. At high-binge colleges, 26 percent of women reported an unwanted sexual advance in connection with others' alcohol use, compared to 15 percent of women at low-binge campuses.

A NEW APPROACH TO AN OLD PROBLEM

All colleges are unique; each has its own culture and traditions, resources and priorities, and relationship with the local community. But every college with a substantial proportion of binge drinkers must begin with the question "Can we accomplish our mission and fulfill our students' goals if we tolerate behavior that compromises the quality of students' educational and social lives, as well as their health and safety?" If that question leads to a commitment to act vigorously and systematically against campus alcohol abuse, multiple approaches tailored to conditions on each campus will certainly be needed. The following "Twelve-Step Program" provides a model that colleges can adapt to their own needs.

1. *Assess the ways in which alcohol is affecting your college.* Everyone, from the college president down, is susceptible to denial about the extent of a college's alcohol abuse problem and its impact on the life of the campus. . . .

2. *Admit that your college has an alcohol problem.* Over the years, many administrations have opted to keep a low profile on their prevention efforts. Denial, a sense of futility, and lack of resources may be at play, but there are other reasons as well. Some administrators fear that a more visible, university-wide stance might create the appearance that alcohol abuse is unusually severe at their school, ignoring the possibility that the college might instead be viewed as mounting a realistic, systematic response to a common problem other colleges prefer to sweep under the rug. Some institutions' legal counsels may advise doing as little as possible that might suggest knowledge of an alcohol problem or acceptance of any responsibility for the environment that encourages it. But the prevalence of binge drinking on campus is no secret, and it is difficult to see how a college administrator could successfully claim not to know it exists.

LONG-TERM STRATEGIES

3. *A systematic effort begins with the president.* Commitment and leadership at the top are vital to assure that consistent, long-term prevention and intervention strategies are reflected not just in speeches but in budgets. To be sure, on some campuses officials are making great efforts to reduce alcohol abuse. At others, however, they seem oblivious to the magnitude and effects of the abuse. They seem to believe that this deep-seated American problem can be changed by an able and dedicated staffer working part-time in a basement office at the student health service, who has the authority to match the office.

4. *Plan for a long-term effort.* Binge drinking has been present on the American college campus since colonial days and will not disappear overnight. At least one four-year cycle is needed at any college before changes can occur. Frequently, excessive drinking is entrenched in the culture of the campus. . . .

CAMPUS AND COMMUNITY INVOLVEMENT

5. *Involve everyone in the solution.* Every sector of the college community should be involved in developing a response to the alcohol problem. This includes those groups such as health services, security, and administration that usually take part, as well as those that seldom do—athletic departments and faculty members. Colleges and universities offer our most formidable aggregations of specialists in human and organizational behavior, including psychologists, sociologists and anthropologists, linguists and lawyers, teachers and marketing strategists, experts in health and addictions, policy analysts and security specialists, community organizers, family therapists, and systems analysts. Yet it is the rare institution that convenes a working group of appropriately diverse problem-solvers to address the alcohol abuse in its midst. These faculty members can be asked to play a limited but meaningful role in planning and assessment, supporting students and administrators in a campuswide effort.

Athletic directors and coaches can have enormous influence on the drinking culture of a campus, but they are rarely pressed to use it. The very visible example set by athletes, the drinking policy at games, the money showered on campus by the beer industry—all can make some student affairs directors feel they are bailing water with a spoon.

Resident advisors (RAs) and academic and retention counselors have been underutilized. They could enhance both prevention and early intervention efforts, but they each need clear roles. RAs cannot be expected to be both monitors and confidants. They need much better, sustained training and supervision than they typically receive and better support, including the sure protection of explicit policy.

Security officers could also benefit from dedicated training and regular consultation around alcohol-related issues and infractions. It's easy for security staff to lapse into feeling as though they are hurting rather than helping students whose abusive drinking they report to the authorities. Students themselves must carry much of the responsibility for campus change. Student government leaders, peer educators, and campus media can all agree that students are in favor of good times but not in favor of drunkenness.

6. *Involve the local community in your efforts.* Local merchants often supply alcohol to underage students and use marketing strategies offering large volumes of alcohol for cut-rate prices. In turn, student drunkenness often disrupts and damages the local community. Work together with local officials: "Control your al-

cohol providers and we'll control our students." State and local officials must enforce underage drinking laws and strengthen other laws that help limit supply.

An even more important target are the bars and clubs that encourage drunkenness by promoting discount drinks and contests. These clubs often form the nucleus of the advertising in campus newspapers. Colleges will have to exert the power they have to influence the way these clubs operate and are regulated; our institutions are far from helpless or ignorant in these matters. If colleges want to target heavy drinking, drunkenness, and their resulting antisocial behaviors, campus security and town police should be on the same team, working together. In return, colleges can help local law enforcement agencies by providing more consistent disciplinary policies for students whose drunken behavior violates the law.

PROVIDING AN ENVIRONMENT CONDUCIVE TO LEARNING

7. *Establish the rights of non-binging students.* Protect non-bingers from the secondhand effects of binge drinking. These student have the right to enjoy a quality of life free from the annoyance and physical harm that stem from the alcohol abuse of others. Encourage the non-bingers by spending as much money and effort on their activities as you spend on cleaning up after the binge drinkers.

Most of all, empower students to take the lead. A successful and sustainable campuswide effort depends on the extent to which students are seen as the leaders of their own self-generated code of respectful community behavior—or the targets of it. Process is not just important, but crucial. It requires patience, persistence, and humility to enable students to take the lead in making drunkenness an unacceptable excuse for violent and disruptive behavior that violates other students' rights. But a set of policies and exhortations from above simply will not suffice. Students bothered by secondhand binge effects gradually will feel empowered to speak up without feeling humiliated themselves. It will be the students standing at their side and the administrators standing behind them who most contribute to that feeling of empowerment.

We once thought drunk drivers were part of life and smokers had to be tolerated. Today, people feel comfortable speaking out against drunk driving and smoking because we now know the harm those behaviors cause others is not an acceptable price to pay. These same lessons can help students who suffer the secondhand effects of other students' drinking to speak up in protest.

8. *Target disruptive behavior for disciplinary action.* Develop a code of

conduct in concert with non-binging students. Enforce the code strictly. Drunkenness should not be viewed as a mitigating circumstance for antisocial behavior. The key to this nation's intervention efforts may lie in recognizing secondhand binge effects on college campuses. In any system with alcohol abuse, whether a family or a campus, the least effective intervention point is the abuser. By focusing on those who suffer from the secondhand effects of binge drinking, colleges could mobilize millions of students nationwide to assert their right to live free from injury and harm created by the binge drinking of their peers.

Whatever alcohol policies are developed by and for students must be brief and comprehensible enough to be publicized effectively and must be vigorously enforced. It's better to have a few well-specified rules, with teeth, than many intricate rules that students do not read and know will not be enforced.

9. *Address problem drinking at fraternities and sororities.* As pointed out earlier, the single strongest indicator of binge drinking is fraternity or sorority membership. A college that is seriously committed to remedying the situation must confront alcohol abuse in fraternities and sororities and gain alumni support in this effort.

Many fraternities and sororities are functional saloons. Fully 86 percent of men and 80 percent of women who live in fraternities and sororities are binge drinkers. The rare president or dean who tells the Greeks to "shape up or ship out," and then keeps his or her word, earns the respect of many. The national organizations must be held accountable for serving underage students in their houses and providing an environment where binge drinking is the norm.

10. *Provide a full-time education for a full-time tuition.* Hold class on Fridays and require attendance. Schedule Friday exams. A college should not become an enabler for students who binge drink from Thursday to Sunday.

11. *Encourage problem drinkers to seek help or treatment.* Make referral and treatment resources readily available. Train RAs and peers to recognize alcohol problems and to urge problem drinkers to seek help.

12. *Freshman orientation should start long before students arrive on campus.* Many colleges have a "party school" image. Send the message loud and clear: "We do not offer a major in binge drinking." Use the admissions office, high school guidance counselors, the college catalog, and alumni to get this message out.

Change expectations of incoming freshmen before they arrive on campus, since half of college bingers began binging in high school or earlier. Colleges also need to examine the expectations they are planting, or failing to plant, in applicants and entering students. Their promotional material should reflect not just the school's educational and athletic achievements, but the quality of student life—including the measures they are willing to take to safeguard it. Recruiters can be trained to describe an institution as a place where there are a great many ways to have a good time, but where drunken behavior is decidedly unwelcome. By taking these active steps to change its image, the institution can be expected eventually to improve its drinking culture, probably upgrade its academic standing, and save some of the costs associated with alcohol abuse.

At some campuses, freshman orientation is something between a lost opportunity and a week-long drunk. When they first arrive on campus—usually before other students—many freshmen will respond positively to initiatives they would later spurn, particularly if the initiatives represent an opportunity to meet their classmates under relatively natural conditions.

First-year women students need special attention. Many have had little experience with alcohol abuse in high school and need to understand that because of the differences in metabolism women cannot drink equally with men. It only takes four drinks for a woman to begin having the same alcohol-related problems as a man who has five drinks. And women's risk of sexual assault, unwanted pregnancy, and exposure to HIV and other sexually transmitted diseases is dramatically increased by the alcohol abuse of their companions, as well as by their own drinking.

Remember, there are no easy solutions or magic bullets for alcohol abuse. Only a comprehensive, concerted, multifaceted, and wide-sweeping effort utilizing all parts of the college community can be expected to have an effect on this long-standing and deeply entrenched problem.

"Nothing will stop [repeat drunk drivers] from operating a motor vehicle under the influence except imprisonment and an intensive substance abuse program."

INCARCERATION AND TREATMENT SHOULD BE USED TO COMBAT DRUNK DRIVING

Leonard Zailskas

Leonard Zailskas is the founder of the Braintree Alternative Center Substance Abuse Program, a treatment facility for repeat drunk drivers in Massachusetts. In the following viewpoint, Zailskas argues that repeat drunk drivers are typically alcoholics with social and psychological problems. In order to protect society from the potential damage such individuals can do on the road, he contends, repeat drunk drivers should be given significant jail sentences followed by mandatory, intensive alcoholism treatment and aftercare based on the program of Alcoholics Anonymous.

As you read, consider the following questions:

1. Why should repeat drunk drivers spend a minimum of thirty days in jail before being transferred to a treatment program, in the author's opinion?
2. How would longer sentences for drunk drivers improve the effectiveness of treatment, according to Zailskas?
3. At what point should repeat drunk drivers lose their licenses, according to the author?

From Leonard Zailskas, "Repeat Drunk Drivers: The Problem and Solution," *American Jails*, May/June 1994. Reprinted by permission of the American Jail Association. (Notes/references in the original have been omitted here.)

Each year on U.S. highways approximately 25,000 lives are lost due to drunk driving. During the ten years of the Vietnam War 58,000 Americans were killed. The comparison is startling—drunk drivers kill almost as many people in one year as were killed in five years of war. According to the Mothers Against Drunk Driving (MADD), 500,000 Americans will be injured in alcohol-related crashes each year. That's about one every minute. In fact, on average, a fatal alcohol-related motor vehicle crash occurs every 22 minutes.

Inspired by groups such as MADD in the early 1980s, legislators realized the seriousness of the drunk driving epidemic and responded by enacting tougher laws. Drunk drivers are now being jailed more frequently and for longer periods of time. Since their numbers in the corrections system increased dramatically, our jails became overcrowded. The most prudent solution to this twofold problem then became the establishment of treatment programs, usually in less secure settings, for repeat drunk drivers (first offenders rarely serve time). Now we were able to study them as a homogeneous group looking for similarities, behavior patterns, and/or unique personality characteristics in an attempt to provide the most effective treatment possible.

One such program is the Braintree Alternative Center (BAC) in Braintree, Massachusetts, which is an alternative placement to the Norfolk County Sheriffs Office and Correctional Center. Established in 1985, it is a 56-bed, state-accredited treatment facility. As of November 1993 more than 2,000 inmates have served time at the BAC.

DISTURBING CHARACTERISTICS

As the founder and Director of the BAC Treatment Program, I have noticed a number of disturbing characteristics concerning this population. Many inmates have completed other substance abuse programs, ranging from eight weeks as an outpatient to months as an inpatient at prestigious centers (e.g., Edgehill, Beech Hill, etc.). Obviously the prior treatment "did not take" as they continued to drink and suffer progressively adverse consequences. Rather than accepting responsibility for drinking and driving, they often portray themselves as victims of an overzealous judicial system. Actually only 1 out of 2,000 drivers with a blood alcohol level of .10 percent, or higher, is arrested. It is estimated that 5,000 miles of alcohol-impaired driving occur for each arrest. With these statistics the judicial system could hardly be described as "overzealous" and, in fact, more resources should be committed to the fight against drunk driving.

In my opinion, many offenders are Type II alcoholics who have a form of genetic alcoholism inherited from their fathers. There is a 90 percent rate of transmission characterized by drinking at an early age, 11 or 12, and rapidly becoming addicted (Type I is less severe and can be inherited by either sex from either parent with onset after age 25). This is evidenced by the younger BAC inmates in their mid-twenties who already have, at a minimum, ten years of alcoholic drinking experience. They swore they would never drink for fear of becoming like their fathers only to succumb to the disease. Their jail sentence is usually their longest period of sobriety. In a related study of alcoholics admitted to treatment for alcoholism, it was discovered that clients with a history of motor vehicle accidents were likely to have initiated regular drinking and heavy drinking at an earlier age.

SOCIAL DRINKERS AND REPEAT OFFENDERS

Since more than 100 million Americans drink regularly, it is understandable that many empathize with those convicted of operating under the influence (OUI). They know that even though they are social drinkers, on at least one occasion, they were probably over the legal alcohol limit. When social drinkers are convicted of OUI and suffer the humiliation of arrest, fines, and outpatient alcohol treatment, they probably would not drink and drive again or at least make sure they did not approach intoxication. For repeat offenders, however, excessive alcohol consumption is a coping mechanism and for many a lifestyle. With repeated episodes of intoxication it is only a matter of time before their destructive behavior leads to trouble with the law. Since many started drinking at an early age they have numerous arrests on their record. In a longitudinal study J. McCord investigated childhood and adolescent antisocial behavior between OUI offenders and nonoffenders. Since the samples were drawn from the same neighborhood, outside causative factors between the groups were minimized. The sample included 36 OUI offenders and 430 nonoffenders.

> Results indicated that the convicted OUI offenders were more likely than the nonoffenders to (1) have been convicted for serious crimes against persons and property; (2) be alcoholic; (3) have had greater exposure to parental conflict and aggression; and (4) have gotten into trouble in adulthood through drinking and the physical expression of anger. Thus, the findings of this longitudinal study of men suggests distinctly different developmental pathways for eventually convicted OUI offender and

nonoffender groups, with the offenders manifesting severe anti-social behaviors and higher rates of alcoholism and alcohol related problems.

According to the National Institute on Alcohol Abuse and Alcoholism (NIAAA), 25 percent of alcoholics have antisocial personality characteristics when only 1.5 percent of the general population qualifies for the diagnosis. In a separate study of 1,406 OUI offenders in Massachusetts, it was found that more than 75 percent had been arraigned for at least one criminal offense and more than 50 percent were arraigned for criminal offenses other than or in addition to their OUI offenses. Also, among OUI recidivists, 68 percent had prior criminal arrests. Repeat OUI offenders should not be viewed as "unlucky social drinkers" but alcoholics with psychosocial difficulties who engage in high-risk behavior and, therefore, pose a serious threat to society.

TREATMENT AND LONGER SENTENCES

Obviously repeat drunk drivers threaten the safety of our roadways. What can be done about it?

First, more treatment programs like the BAC should be established. A 1987 study of a court-mandated treatment facility similar to the BAC reported only a 6 percent recidivism rate as compared to 19 percent for offenders from low-security institutions and an overall rate of 25 percent statewide. Another study of a court-ordered residential treatment program followed 50 alcoholic offenders, who received treatment, for 7 to 9 years. Although 28 percent were convicted of further offenses, 40 percent either partially or completely abstained from alcohol. Since Alcoholics Anonymous "works best for most," in the words of Fr. Martin, it should serve as the treatment base. Transfers to such institutions, however, should be initiated only after the inmate has served a minimum of 30 days in the House of Correction. This prolonged exposure to a harsh environment would provide reality testing, a "wake up call" if you will, to the repeat OUI offenders as well as motivate them to seek a transfer to the minimum security setting of a program. It is in the best interests of society to provide this rehabilitation opportunity as opposed to the strictly retributive approach of "dead time" in jail.

Second, I suggest longer jail sentences starting with the second OUI. It is estimated that 70 percent to 80 percent of people arrested for drunk driving two or more times are alcoholics. According to statistics from the Justice Department, more than half of the 1.7 million Americans arrested for drunken driving in

1989 had already done jail or prison time for OUI. One third of those arrested for drunken driving had served time for OUI three or more times. The current system of short sentences is too lenient and actually enables an offender/alcoholic by prolonging the time it takes before he suffers severe enough consequences to seek help. Currently, when parole is denied in a short sentence it is viewed as a mere inconvenience. With longer sentences parole takes on new meaning. Inmates would be highly motivated to participate in the treatment program in order to earn a parole. Longer sentences mean longer exposure to treatment which is necessary to penetrate their characteristic thick denial, and alcoholism, like any disease, can be more easily arrested the earlier it is detected and treated. Due to the effects of postacute withdrawal longer treatment programs will stabilize the individual physically and psychologically. When he begins thinking clearly he will be in a better position to integrate the essentials of living a sober life.

Pat McCarthy. Reprinted by permission of the artist.

Third, since it is estimated that 75 percent of those whose licenses have been suspended or revoked continue to drive it is necessary to lengthen the mandator sentences of those convicted of Driving After Revocation. Instead of serving only 60 days, a minimum mandatory of 120 days or more should be instituted. The penalty must be severe in order for it to truly function as a deterrent.

Fourth, after a conviction for a fourth OUI within the last 10 years there should be a mandatory loss of license for at least 10 years and lifetime license revocation for a fifth OUI.

AFTERCARE

Fifth, there should be a highly structured aftercare program for those completing the treatment program which should include:

(a) Probation/parole officers specifically trained in alcoholism that deal exclusively with repeat OUI offenders. Currently OUI offenders are considered "light weights" compared to the hardened criminals on their caseloads and usually don't command the time and attention of their counterparts.

(b) Completion of an aftercare program as a stipulation of probation or parole. Failure to comply with aftercare regulations means an immediate return to incarceration.

(c) Random drug and alcohol screening tests to assure abstinence.

(d) A mixture of mandatory supervised A.A. meetings which includes 12-Step, Big Book, and Open Discussion meetings in addition to Open Speaker meetings. The four types of meetings broaden the range of A.A. offerings in hopes that at least one type will be attractive enough for the offender to attend voluntarily upon completion of his court-ordered obligation.

(e) Substance abuse group therapy and education at least once a week.

(f) Mandatory family involvement in the treatment process to better equip the family to deal with their substance abuser. Al-Anon participation should be encouraged with on-site meetings if possible.

COERCION IS NECESSARY

I realize A.A. is strictly voluntary and that my proposal is not in keeping with A.A. tradition. Critics would also point out that you can't force someone into treatment. A pioneer in the alcoholism field, Fr. Martin, was asked, "Is it true that you cannot help an alcoholic unless he wants help?" His response, "That's a lie. It's a myth. I know the saying that you can lead a horse to water but you can't make him drink. But I say you could lead him to a well and make him thirsty. That's what we do when we coerce an alcoholic into treatment. We offer him something to respond to. If the treatment is good he will probably respond."

Did the overwhelming majority of A.A. participants awake

one sunny morning and have a sudden urge to attend their very first A.A. meeting? More than likely the alcoholic attends his first meeting because of coercion from his wife, employer, the courts, etc., as a result of alcohol-induced destructive behavior. Repeat drunk drivers obviously have not responded to the initial pressure to become abstinent so a more powerful, structured approach is necessary. According to Mary F. O'Connell, an alcohol/drug counselor working with OUI offenders, "The combination of imposing sanctions and mandatory substance abuse education works for some people. But for those who continue drinking after such treatment, nothing will stop them from operating a motor vehicle under the influence except imprisonment and an intensive substance abuse program."

"We must continue to galvanize public anger about the problem of alcohol-impaired driving."

MEDIA CAMPAIGNS CAN EFFECTIVELY COMBAT DRUNK DRIVING

William DeJong and Charles K. Atkin

William DeJong is a lecturer in the Department of Health and Social Behavior at the Harvard School of Public Health in Boston, Massachusetts. Charles K. Atkin is a professor of communication at the College of Communication Arts and Science at Michigan State University in East Lansing, Michigan. In the following viewpoint, DeJong and Atkin describe attempts to prevent alcohol-impaired driving by means of televised public service announcements (PSAs). The authors contend that although these PSAs have had some success, a more comprehensive media effort is needed in order to win more support for public policies designed to discourage drunk driving.

As you read, consider the following questions:

1. What three types of objectives do mass communication campaigns promote, according to the authors?
2. What four points do the authors say should be underscored by future mass media campaigns?
3. What two alternatives to PSAs do DeJong and Atkin recommend?

From William DeJong and Charles K. Atkin, "A Review of National Television PSA Campaigns for Preventing Alcohol-Impaired Driving, 1987-1992," *Journal of Public Health Policy*, vol. 16, no. 1, Spring 1995. Reprinted with permission. (Notes/references in the original have been omitted here.)

Public service announcements (PSAs) aired on television have long been a central part of our nation's effort to prevent alcohol-impaired driving. Analysts have noted that there is little evidence that such campaigns significantly alter people's drinking and driving behavior. In fact, evaluations of PSA campaigns are rare, partly due to the expense, but also due to the difficulty of setting up a research design that permits meaningful inferences about a campaign's impact.

Even so, we expect many advocates to continue looking to PSAs as a critical weapon in the crusade against alcohol-impaired driving. With that prospect in view, it is essential to take a step back, analyze the PSAs that have been done in recent years, and then plan a more effective use of this media resource. . . .

We reviewed a total of 137 PSAs [that aired nationally on U.S. television between 1987 and 1992] from the following sources (the number of PSAs from each is in brackets): American Broadcasting Company [7]; Columbia Broadcasting System [52]; Harvard Alcohol Project, Harvard School of Public Health [6]; Mothers Against Drunk Driving, Irving, TX [34]; National Broadcasting Company [6]; Project TEAM (Techniques for Effective Alcohol Management), Washington, DC [21]; and U.S. Department of Transportation (USDOT), in collaboration with the Advertising Council [11]. . . .

Mass communication campaigns can be used to promote a wide range of objectives, which we can divide into three basic types: 1) general awareness, 2) individual behavior change, and 3) public action. PSAs aired between 1987 and 1992 focused on the first two objectives, with little attention given to building public support for changes in institutional structures, public policy or law that would reinforce and sustain the efforts of individuals to alter their behavior.

GENERAL AWARENESS

General awareness PSAs are designed to increase public recognition of a problem and establish it as a primary concern. Several of MADD's PSAs were designed to accomplish this objective. In a 1990 spot, for example, the announcer stated MADD's case as follows: "If we can save the whales, and save the dolphins, how come we can't do the same thing for children?"

Many of MADD's spots addressed the audience as potential perpetrators, usually concluding with simple appeals not to drink and drive. Sometimes this appeal was appended to a poignant story about a victim or a recitation of alcohol-impaired driving statistics. In other cases, the approach was lighter. In "Visions of Summer," for example, there was a montage of summer scenes, from children running through a sprinkler to a pick-up basketball game. As a red, hazy sun set over a hillock, the announcer said, "Keep it a safe summer. Please, don't drink and drive."

ALTERING PATTERNS AND SAVING LIVES

The relative ineffectiveness of existing deterrence-based countermeasures [to fight drunk driving] has prompted calls to consider alternative strategies based in a broader understanding of the roots of drinking and driving. In particular, commentators have suggested that drunk driving is best conceptualized not as a criminal justice problem but as a social problem. From a social problems perspective, drunk driving and the annual toll it exacts are seen as the inevitable result of the intersection of central American social institutions: transportation and recreation.

As H. Laurence Ross points out, this institutional approach—what he refers to as the "challenging paradigm"—leads to two important policy implications. First, unlike a criminal justice approach, the main emphasis should not be on catching and punishing (or even reforming) drunk drivers. Instead, the focus should be on altering institutional patterns, especially those that foster the intersection of automobile use and alcohol consumption. Second, drunk driving is seen as a public health issue; and as with other health problems, the goal should be to devise policies that save lives and reduce injuries. Criminal justice sanctions can be applied only to the culpable (even if general deterrence is hoped for) and often are applied only after substantial harm has occurred. Lifesaving countermeasures, however, can be implemented across the population and are concerned with prevention.

Brandon K. Applegate et al., *Crime & Delinquency*, April 1995.

One concern about the "don't drink and drive" message is that, if taken literally, some people might view it as extreme and unrealistic, given the current social climate, their own experience with driving after drinking, and the lack of consensus among policy experts on whether small amounts of alcohol consumption play a significant causative role in traffic crashes.

General awareness PSAs are also intended to help change the meaning of driving after drinking and thereby facilitate a shift in social norms. To this end, MADD frequently emphasized that alcohol-impaired driving is the result of someone's decision to drive after drinking. In "Classroom," for example, a stern child was shown supervising a class of adult pupils as they wrote on the blackboard over and over again, "Drunk driving is not an accident."

INDIVIDUAL BEHAVIOR CHANGE

An important objective for several PSAs was to encourage individuals to change their behavior to avoid driving after drinking. A useful framework for understanding how to accomplish this objective comes from the communication/behavior change model, which elaborates the steps in the behavior change process that can be addressed through mass media: 1) increasing knowledge and changing beliefs that impede behavior change; 2) modeling new behavioral skills; 3) showing how barriers to change can be overcome; 4) teaching self-management techniques to sustain behavior change; and 5) demonstrating social support for that change.

An implication of this model is that simple exhortations not to drink and drive, by failing to promote specific alternative behaviors, are unlikely to have broad impact. Such messages do offer supportive arguments that might increase knowledge and change beliefs, but this is likely to stimulate new behaviors among only a small group of people already predisposed to change.

There are three types of specific behaviors that the PSAs promote: 1) designating a driver, 2) intervening to prevent alcohol-impaired people from driving, and 3) calling for additional information or to enroll in prevention activities. . . .

PUBLIC ACTION

A third key objective of mass media campaigns is to stimulate and support public action to address a problem. One form of public action is the formation and effective implementation of school- or community-based programs. In this case, PSAs can be used to position a program or organization as a leader in combatting the problem of alcohol-impaired driving; to recruit new program participants, volunteers, or donors; to maintain the morale of people already involved; and to announce program activities.

Both MADD and Project TEAM had spots designed to accomplish these objectives. MADD often used Connie Sellecca to promote its Project Red Ribbon, for which people are asked to tie a red ribbon to their car as a symbol of their commitment to drive sober. Similarly, TEAM had two "TEAM Spirit" spots that were designed to introduce its program for encouraging responsible alcohol consumption at sports stadiums.

Public action can also entail working for changes in public policy. The 1989 Surgeon General's Workshop on Drunk Driving led to several recommendations for policy change, such as reducing the legal *per se* limit [the illegal level of blood alcohol content (BAC)] to .08% BAC, expanding the use of sobriety checkpoints, reforming alcohol advertising, and increasing alcohol excise taxes. Promoting such measures is critical, for by changing the overall social, legal, and economic environment, people will be led to take a variety of steps to avoid driving after drinking.

In general, the spots we reviewed did not work to achieve any specific changes in public policy. Several spots, especially those from MADD, emphasized the terrible death toll caused by alcohol-impaired driving. This would serve to generate pressure for something to be done, but what that might be was never specified. The reason for this is straightforward: Many broadcasters elect not to air this type of message as a PSA. As we explain below, there are other ways to use PSAs to promote policy change, short of listing specific legislation or regulatory proposals. There is also the option of using paid advertising instead of seeking donated public service time.

Once changes in public policy are made, PSAs can play a critical role in publicizing them so that they can have their full deterrent effect. The national campaigns we reviewed did not include any PSAs of this type. Even vague references to strict law enforcement were rare. In a MADD spot, after viewers saw a man arrested for alcohol-impaired driving, the announcer said, "We think it's only fair to remind you that almost one thousand new laws have been passed to guarantee, if you don't appoint a designated driver, one will be appointed for you." A CBS spot took a similar tack, stating, "A drunk driving arrest can cost thousands of dollars in attorney's fees, fines, and increased auto insurance. Choosing a designated driver costs nothing." Many state and local campaigns, it should be noted, have made the risk of arrest and its legal and financial consequences a central feature of their messages. . . .

TOWARD A COMMON PLAN OF APPROACH

At a 1971 conference on public information programs on alcohol and highway safety, several experts pointed to the need for greater coordination among campaigns against alcohol-impaired driving. We see that same need today.

From 1987 to 1992 there was an overemphasis on promoting the designated driver concept at the expense of several additional prevention messages that the public needs. In part, this reflected the success of the Harvard Alcohol Project in convincing the three major television networks to develop and air their own PSAs on this subject. Actually, it was easy for broadcasters to embrace this approach, since it did not threaten the vital interests of their beer and wine sponsors. In our view, there was yet another factor at work here: the tendency of government and public service organizations concerned about alcohol-impaired driving to work independently, with little sharing of plans.

We therefore offer the following recommendations with the hope that they will encourage key prevention groups to develop a common plan of approach. We first present recommendations concerning the content of future mass media campaigns. It is our view that these campaigns should be refocused to promote not just individual action, but *public action* as well.

With this focus, television PSAs will be able to play only a limited role. Because the broadcast industry will work to preserve its profits from alcohol advertising, this will remain the case until so-called "counter-advertising" is mandated by law, a proposal put forth by the Surgeon General's Workshop on Drunk Driving. We therefore conclude with a call for greater use of media advocacy strategies, including paid radio advertising.

REINFORCING A SHIFT IN SOCIAL NORMS

A key to getting further reductions in alcohol-related traffic fatalities is to reinforce an emerging shift in U.S. social norms against alcohol-impaired driving. Truly, the last decade has seen tremendous progress on this front, largely due to the efforts of MADD and other grassroots organizations. As a result, alcohol-impaired driving is no longer a source of easy laughs, nor is it shrugged off as an inevitable cost of modern life. Still, much more needs to be done.

This effort to change social norms should proceed on two fronts. First, we must continue to galvanize public anger about the problem of alcohol-impaired driving. To understand why, consider the case of tobacco smoking. While smoking was once widely viewed as a sexy, glamorous habit, today it is increasingly viewed as a sign of poor self-discipline and callous disregard for other people. Indeed, to be a smoker now is to carry the weight of *stigma*.

The notion of stigma is one that has been explored at length by social scientists. Erving Goffman, who defined a stigma as any attribute that is deeply discrediting to its possessor, identified three types: 1) physical deformities, 2) tribal stigmata (e.g., race, religion, social class), and 3) characterological stigmata, or those that betray a flaw in character. Any stigma with its roots in character has two defining attributes. First, the behavior that reveals the supposed flaw in character is perceived to be under voluntary control. Second, that behavior has important negative consequences for others.

Being a smoker currently meets both of these defining conditions. First, smoking is perceived to be voluntarily adopted and maintained. While the impediments to quitting are well-known, the public also knows that millions of smokers with sufficient will power have quit smoking. Second, recent data on the effects of "environmental tobacco smoke" have demonstrated to people that the smokers around them are putting their own health at risk. With that, the non-smokers' rights movement gained full force; at the root of that movement is anger.

STIGMATIZING ALCOHOL-IMPAIRED DRIVING

This suggests that to stigmatize alcohol-impaired driving, we must ensure that the public sees clearly that this behavior emerges from a series of choices that the driver has made. Beyond that, we must keep the public focused on the consequences that drinking and driving by others might have for them and their loved ones. That is, we must address members of the public, not as potential perpetrators, but as *potential victims* of impaired driving.

Efforts to stigmatize alcohol-impaired driving should focus not only on the "drunk driver," but also on the alcohol industry itself, which earns tremendous profits from sales to problem drinkers who are at risk for impaired driving. Those who drive after drinking are making bad choices, but they are induced to do so by a social, legal, and economic environment that promotes excessive consumption. This environment is molded by the industry through its marketing and advertising strategies and through its political clout, which stifles policy reform.

ATTACKING THE SYSTEM OF BELIEFS

On a second front, we must attack the existing system of knowledge and beliefs that operate to sustain current drinking and driving norms. We must move our target audiences from their emotional reaction to specific victims' stories to a rational consideration of the nature and scope of the problem. We propose that future mass media campaigns underscore the following points:

1) The phrase "drunk driving accident" obscures the cause-and-effect relationship between driving after drinking and mo-

tor vehicle crashes. An alcohol-related crash is the predictable result of someone's decision to drive after drinking, a decision for which they must be held accountable.

2) Every act of impaired driving puts other lives at risk. Hence, the very act of impaired driving is a serious offense, whether it happens to result in a crash or not.

3) Many drivers, especially teens and young adults, underestimate their degree of impairment and its impact on their driving skills.

4) The risk of causing a motor vehicle crash is greatly magnified even at BAC levels as low as .05 percent. The current *per se* limit of .10 percent BAC represents an extremely dangerous level of impairment.

CHANNELING PUBLIC ANGER INTO DEMANDS FOR POLICY CHANGE

The fear of causing death or injury and the threat of strong social disapproval will continue to motivate responsible behavior among many drivers, especially those who typically drink in moderation. But to reach problem drinkers, we must concentrate on changing the social, legal and economic environment in which people make decisions about their drinking and driving behavior.

To effect these changes, public anger about the toll exacted by alcohol-impaired drivers must be channeled into demands for action from public officials. Such a campaign was undertaken in the late 1960s by Allstate Insurance. Linked to a high-profile television campaign, one series of Allstate print ads presented coupons that readers could send to their governor or state legislators to demand new laws that would be consistent with USDOT recommendations.

Several changes in public policy should be advocated through future mass media campaigns. First, there must be effective, well-financed, and sustained law enforcement, punctuated by the frequent and well-publicized use of "sobriety checkpoints." The key here is not to be found in boosting the severity of punishment for the small minority of impaired drivers who are arrested each year, but in increasing the public's perception of the likelihood of detection and punishment.

Second, there needs to be increased local control of alcohol availability, primarily through stricter enforcement of existing laws to stop the sale and distribution of alcohol to minors. The uniform minimum drinking age of 21 has made a dramatic difference in reducing alcohol-related traffic deaths, but the impact of this law is undermined through lackadaisical enforcement.

New Legislation and Increased Taxes

Third, we need new legislation passed to deter alcohol-impaired driving. A top priority is to decrease the *per se* limit to .08% BAC for adults, even lower (e.g., .02% BAC) for minors. This policy is endorsed by USDOT, MADD, and many other organizations. Another priority is administrative license revocation, which allows the prompt removal of a driver's license if the driver is tested and found to have a BAC higher than the legal limit.

Fourth, as a means to reduce alcohol consumption and thereby reduce mortality and morbidity due to alcohol-impaired driving, excise taxes on alcohol should be further increased, with future increases indexed to inflation. This is an especially important strategy for deterring youth alcohol consumption, due to their greater price sensitivity. Beer and wine should be taxed at the same level by ethanol content as distilled spirits.

Television PSAs can play an important but somewhat limited role in this advocacy effort, even if broadcasters refuse to air spots that make a direct and specific appeal for policy change. First, a PSA can provide factual information that will bolster public receptivity to proposals announced through press conferences and other means. For example, the need for a lower *per se* limit could be substantiated by a PSA that shows how driving is severely impaired at BAC levels far lower than the standard U.S. limit of .10%. Second, a PSA can position the sponsoring organization as an agent of change. Through a hotline number, callers can get a fact sheet of information on various public policy proposals or learn how to get more involved in fighting for change.

Moving Beyond Television PSAs

While television PSAs have been the primary focus of this viewpoint, we should not forget the importance of other media strategies for reaching the public with effective, policy-oriented messages. We offer two recommendations.

First, we urge the greater use of radio, which has been underutilized in previous campaigns. Radio, like television, is a good medium for providing short, uncomplicated messages, evoking emotional reactions, establishing evidence of new social norms, and modeling behaviors that can be easily taught. In addition, the variety of stations on the air makes it easier to target messages to specific, well-defined audiences.

A chief advantage of radio, however, is its lower costs compared to television, both in terms of production and advertising rates. This makes the strategy of using paid advertising a real possibility. Paid radio ads, coupled with press events and grassroots organizing, are a powerful tool for advancing legislation.

Second, we echo the call for prevention advocates to make more extensive use of "media advocacy" strategies. The media advocacy approach does not focus on promoting individual behavior change, but on highlighting the role of important political and economic interests in shaping an environment that promotes unhealthful behavior choices. Action-oriented media advocacy is especially effective for putting the spotlight on legislators and other officials who can bring about policy change.

In practice, media advocacy involves paid advertising plus a variety of strategies for stimulating news media coverage, all of which is designed to reframe how the general public and opinion leaders conceptualize a public health problem and to promote a consideration of public policy options. In contrast to public education campaigns, media advocacy techniques are flexible and responsive, yet relatively inexpensive to implement.

BUILDING SUPPORT FOR CHANGE

We recommend that future mass media campaigns against alcohol-impaired driving focus on building support for changes in institutional structures, public policy, or law that will motivate, support, and sustain the efforts of individuals to alter their behavior. Television PSAs will be an important but limited part of these future campaigns. Greater emphasis should be given instead to media advocacy strategies, including paid radio advertising. We further recommend that the principal organizations concerned about alcohol-impaired driving share their plans and develop a common communications strategy that will advance the public policy agenda proposed by the Surgeon General's Workshop on Drunk Driving.

PERIODICAL BIBLIOGRAPHY

The following articles have been selected to supplement the diverse views presented in this chapter. Addresses are provided for periodicals not indexed in the *Readers' Guide to Periodical Literature*, the *Alternative Press Index*, the *Social Sciences Index*, or the *Index to Legal Periodicals and Books*.

Colman Andrews	"In Defense Of: Getting Drunk," *Los Angeles Times Magazine*, January 2, 1994. Available from Times Mirror Square, Los Angeles, CA 90053.
Brandon K. Applegate et al.	"Public Support for Drunk-Driving Countermeasures: Social Policy for Saving Lives," *Crime and Delinquency*, April 1995.
Doug Bandow	"This Is a Crusade That Is in No One's Interest," *Conservative Chronicle*, March 10, 1993. Available from Box 37077, Boone, IA 50037-0077.
Mike Brake	"Needed: A License to Drink," *Newsweek*, March 14, 1994.
Robert D. Brewer et al.	"The Risk of Dying in Alcohol-Related Automobile Crashes Among Habitual Drunk Drivers," *New England Journal of Medicine*, August 25, 1994. Available from 10 Shattuck St., Boston, MA 02115-6094.
Julie Candler	"A Sobering Law for Truckers," *Nation's Business*, January 1996.
William Celis III	"Tradition on the Wane: College Drinking," *New York Times*, February 5, 1995.
Simin Liu et al.	"Prevalence of Alcohol-Impaired Driving: Results from a National Self-Reported Survey of Health Behaviors," *JAMA*, January 8, 1997. Available from 515 N. State St., Chicago, IL 60610.
Willard G. Manning et al.	"The Taxes of Sin: Do Smokers and Drinkers Pay Their Way?" *JAMA*, March 17, 1989.
Richard A. McGowan	"Lotteries and Sin Taxes: Painless Revenue or Painful Mirage?" *America*, April 30, 1994.
Ellen Perlman	"Moving Toward None for the Road," *Governing*, September 1994.
Robert W. Stock	"Alcohol Lures the Old," *New York Times*, April 18, 1996.
Elizabeth M. Whelan	"Perils of Prohibition: Why We Should Lower the Drinking Age to 18," *Newsweek*, May 29, 1995.

FOR FURTHER DISCUSSION

CHAPTER 1

1. Curtis Ellison and Albert B. Lowenfels both acknowledge the health benefits as well as the risks associated with drinking alcohol, but Ellison emphasizes the benefits while Lowenfels focuses on the risks. Each author cites scientific sources to support his arguments. Which author's use of such information is more effective? Explain your answer.

2. Dave Shiflett argues that alcoholic beverage producers should be allowed to promote the health benefits of moderate drinking. George A. Hacker insists that this policy would result in an increase in alcohol consumption and abuse. Which author's argument is more persuasive? Why?

3. All of the authors in this chapter acknowledge that drinking moderate amounts of alcohol reduces the risk for coronary heart disease in some individuals. However, they disagree about whether this information justifies recommending alcohol to nondrinkers. Which authors favor such a policy? Do any authors favor a blanket recommendation that all nondrinkers start drinking? Summarize each author's position on this issue.

CHAPTER 2

1. Fred A. Meister is the president and CEO of the Distilled Spirits Council of the United States, an organization that represents the liquor industry. Does knowing his background influence your assessment of his argument that advertising liquor on television and radio is not irresponsible? Explain your answer. Does knowing that such advertising is opposed by the American Medical Association, the nation's largest association of physicians, influence your opinion on this issue? Explain your answer.

2. John Leo suggests that allowing liquor ads to air on television could result in an increase in alcohol consumption by young people. Morris E. Chafetz contends that banning such ads would more likely result in alcohol abuse by young people. Whose argument do you find more persuasive? Why?

3. Diana P. Hackbarth, Barbara Silvestri, and William Cosper conclude that minority neighborhoods are more likely to have billboards "hawking dangerous products," including alcohol, than are white neighborhoods. Noel N. Hankin argues that such billboards are not the cause of the problems minority

communities experience. What does he say are the causes of crime and violence in the black community? Is his argument convincing? Why or why not? Does knowing that Hankin is the director of corporate relations for the Miller Brewing Company affect your assessment of his contentions? Why or why not?

Chapter 3

1. Terence T. Gorski and Audrey Kishline both agree that the disease concept of alcoholism has been overgeneralized and that some problem drinkers are incorrectly diagnosed as having a disease. However, Gorski contends that the disease label is appropriate for certain types of alcoholics whereas Kishline maintains that alcoholism is not a biological disease. Based on the information presented in the two viewpoints, which author's evaluation of the disease concept of alcoholism seems most credible? Defend your answer with examples from the viewpoints.

2. Several of the viewpoints in this chapter discuss Alcoholics Anonymous (AA), the primary self-help organization for alcoholics. Which viewpoints are supportive of AA and which are critical? Taken altogether, do the arguments in favor of AA outweigh the arguments against it? Explain.

Chapter 4

1. Donald S. Kenkel argues that raising alcohol taxes could result in a decrease in alcohol-related social problems. Dwight B. Heath maintains that such tax increases would punish responsible drinkers while doing nothing to affect the drinking habits of problem drinkers, who are the cause of most alcohol-related problems. Which author is more convincing? Why?

2. Alexander C. Wagenaar and Mark Wolfson contend that minimum drinking-age laws should be enforced more vigorously. William F. Buckley Jr. insists that such laws are futile because young people between eighteen and twenty-one—specifically college students—are likely to drink regardless of the law. Based on your reading of these viewpoints, do you think laws banning those under twenty-one from drinking should be strictly enforced? Why or why not?

3. This chapter describes several approaches to the prevention of alcohol-related problems—especially drunk driving. List these approaches in order of effectiveness. Defend your ranking, using examples from the viewpoints.

ORGANIZATIONS TO CONTACT

The editors have compiled the following list of organizations concerned with the issues debated in this book. The descriptions are derived from materials provided by the organizations. All have publications or information available for interested readers. The list was compiled on the date of publication of the present volume; names, addresses, phone and fax numbers, and e-mail and Internet addresses may change. Be aware that many organizations take several weeks or longer to respond to inquiries, so allow as much time as possible.

Addiction Research Foundation / Fondation de la recherche sur la toxicomanie
33 Russell St., Toronto, ON M5S 2S1, CANADA
(416) 595-6111 • (800) 357-2916 • fax: (416) 595-5017
e-mail: isd@arf.org • Internet: http://www.arf.org
The foundation is devoted to the discovery of new addiction treatments and the creation of addiction-prevention programs. It publishes informational materials for the public and educational products for addiction professionals, including videos, books, and the bimonthly newspaper *Journal*.

Against Drunk Driving (ADD)
PO Box 397 Station A, Brampton, ON L6V 2L3, CANADA
(905) 793-4233 • fax: (905) 793-4233
e-mail: add@netcom.ca • Internet: http://www.netmediapro.com/add
Against Drunk Driving is a Canadian volunteer organization dedicated to reducing death and injury resulting from alcohol-impaired driving. ADD publishes the newsletter *Operation Lookout Network* annually, the newsletter *The ADDvisor* twice a year, and the pamphlet *The Grieving Process*.

Al-Anon Family Group Headquarters
1600 Corporate Landing Pkwy., Virginia Beach, VA 23454
(757) 563-1600 • fax: (757) 563-1655
Internet: http://www.al/anon.alateen.org
Al-Anon is a fellowship of men, women, and children whose lives have been affected by an alcoholic family member or friend. Members share their experiences, strength, and hope to help each other and perhaps to aid in the recovery of the alcoholic. Al-Anon Family Group Headquarters provides information on its local chapters and on its affiliated organization, Alateen. Its publications include the monthly magazine the *Forum*, the semiannual *Al-Anon Speaks Out*, the bimonthly *Alateen Talk*, and several books, including *How Al-Anon Works*, *Path to Recovery: Steps, Traditions, and Concepts*, and *Courage to Be Me: Living with Alcoholism*.

Alcoholics Anonymous (AA)
General Service Office
PO Box 459, Grand Central Station, New York, NY 10163
(212) 870-3400 • fax: (212) 870-3003
Internet: http://www.aa.org

Alcoholics Anonymous is an international fellowship of people who are recovering from alcoholism. Because AA's primary goal is to help alcoholics remain sober, it does not sponsor research or engage in education about alcoholism. AA does, however, publish a catalog of literature concerning the organization as well as several pamphlets, including *Is AA for You? Young People and AA*, and *A Brief Guide to Alcoholics Anonymous*.

American Council on Alcohol Problems (ACAP)
3426 Bridgeland Dr., Bridgeton, MO 63044
(314) 739-5944 • fax: (314) 739-0848

ACAP is the successor to temperance organizations such as the American Temperance League and the Anti-Saloon League. It is composed of state temperance organizations, religious bodies, and fraternal organizations that support ACAP's philosophy of abstinence from alcohol. ACAP works to restrict the availability of alcohol in the United States by controlling alcohol advertising and by educating the public about the harmfulness of alcohol. It serves as a clearinghouse for information and research materials and publishes the monthly *American Issue* for donors.

Canadian Centre on Substance Abuse/Centre canadien de lutte contre l'alcoolisme et les toxicomanies (CCSA/CCLAT)
75 Albert St., Suite 300, Ottawa ON K1P 5E7, CANADA
(800) 214-4788 • (613) 235-4048 • fax: (613) 235-8101
Internet: http://www.ccsa.ca

A Canadian clearinghouse on substance abuse, the CCSA/CCLAT works to disseminate information on the nature, extent, and consequences of substance abuse and to support and assist organizations involved in substance abuse treatment, prevention, and educational programming. The CCSA/CCLAT publishes several books, including *Canadian Profile: Alcohol, Tobacco, and Other Drugs*, as well as reports, policy documents, brochures, research papers, and the newsletter *Action News*.

Distilled Spirits Council of the United States (DISCUS)
1250 I St. NW, Suite 900, Washington, DC 20005
(202) 628-3544

The Distilled Spirits Council of the United States is the national trade association representing producers and marketers of distilled spirits in the United States. It seeks to ensure the responsible advertising and marketing of distilled spirits to adult consumers and to prevent such advertising and marketing from targeting individuals below the legal purchase age. DISCUS publishes fact sheets, the periodic newsletter *News Release*, and several pamphlets, including *The Drunk Driving Prevention Act*.

Entertainment Industries Council (EIC)
1760 Reston Pkwy., Suite 415, Reston, VA 20190-3303
(703) 481-4404 • fax: (703) 481-1418
e-mail: East Coast: eiceast@aol.com • West Coast: eicwest@aol.com

The EIC works to educate the entertainment industry and their audiences about major public health and social issues. Its members strive to effect social change by providing educational materials, research, and training to the entertainment industry. The EIC publishes several fact sheets on alcohol, children of alcoholics, women and addiction, and alcohol-impaired driving.

Mothers Against Drunk Driving (MADD)
511 E. John Carpenter Frwy., No. 700, Irving, TX 75062
(800) GET-MADD (438-6233)
e-mail: Information: info@madd.org • Victim's Assistance:
victims@madd.org • Internet: http://www.madd.org

Mothers Against Drunk Driving seeks to act as the voice of victims of drunk driving accidents by speaking on their behalf to communities, businesses, and educational groups and by providing materials for use in medical facilities and health and driver education programs. MADD publishes the biannual *MADDvocate for Victims Magazine* and the newsletter *MADD in Action* as well as a variety of brochures and other materials on drunk driving.

National Council on Alcoholism and Drug Dependence (NCADD)
12 W. 21st St., New York, NY 10010
(212) 206-6770 • fax: (212) 645-1690
Internet: http://www.ncadd.org

NCADD is a volunteer health organization that helps individuals overcome addictions, advises the federal government on drug and alcohol policies, and develops substance abuse prevention and education programs for youth. It publishes fact sheets, such as *Youth and Alcohol*, and pamphlets, such as *Who's Got the Power? You...or Drugs?*

Office for Substance Abuse Prevention (OSAP)
National Clearinghouse for Alcohol and Drug Information (NCADI)
PO Box 2345, Rockville, MD 20847-2345
(800) 729-6686 • (301) 468-2600
TDD: (800) 487-4889 or (301) 230-2867
Internet: http://www.health.org

OSAP leads U.S. government efforts to prevent alcoholism and other drug problems among Americans. Through the NCADI, OSAP provides the public with a wide variety of information on alcoholism and other addictions. Its publications include the bimonthly *Prevention Pipeline*, the fact sheet *Alcohol Alert*, monographs such as "Social Marketing/Media Advocacy" and "Advertising and Alcohol," brochures, pamphlets, videotapes, and posters. Publications in Spanish are also available.

Rational Recovery Systems (RRS)

PO Box 800, Lotus, CA 95651

(916) 621-4374 • (800) 303-CURE • phone and fax (916) 621-2667

e-mail: Self-Help Network: rrsn@rational.org • Training Institute:
rrti@rational.org • Centers: rrc@rational.org • Political and Legal
Action Network: rrplan@rational.org

Internet: http://www.rational.org/recovery

RRS is a national self-help organization that offers a cognitive rather
than spiritual approach to recovery from alcoholism. Its philosophy
holds that alcoholics can attain sobriety without depending on other
people or a "higher power." Rational Recovery Systems publishes materials about the organization and its use of rational-emotive therapy.

Research Society on Alcoholism (RSA)

4314 Medical Pkwy., No. 300, Austin, TX 78756

phone and fax: (512) 454-0022

e-mail: debbyrsa@bga.com

The RSA provides a forum for researchers who share common interests in alcoholism. The society's purpose is to promote research on the
prevention and treatment of alcoholism. It publishes the journal *Alcoholism: Clinical and Experimental Research* nine times a year as well as the
book series Recent Advances in Alcoholism.

Secular Organizations for Sobriety (SOS)

PO Box 5, Buffalo, NY 14215

(716) 834-2922

SOS is a network of groups dedicated to helping individuals achieve
and maintain sobriety. The organization believes that alcoholics can
best recover by rationally choosing to make sobriety rather than alcohol a priority. Most members of SOS reject the religious basis of Alcoholics Anonymous and other similar self-help groups. SOS publishes
the quarterly *SOS International Newsletter* and distributes the books *Un-
hooked: Staying Sober and Drug Free* and *How to Stay Sober: Recovery Without Religion*,
written by SOS founder James Christopher.

BIBLIOGRAPHY OF BOOKS

Stephen Arterburn

Hand-Me-Down Genes and Second-Hand Emotions: You Can Overcome the Genetic and Family Factors That Can Lead to Depression, Alcoholism, Obesity, and Suicide. New York: Simon & Schuster, 1994.

Henri Begleiter and
Benjamin Kissin

The Genetics of Alcoholism. New York: Oxford University Press, 1995.

Gayle M. Boyd,
Jan Howard, and
Robert A. Zucker, eds.

Alcohol Problems Among Adolescents: Current Directions in Prevention Research. Hillsdale, NJ: Lawrence Erlbaum, 1995.

James Christopher

SOS Sobriety: The Proven Alternative to Twelve-Step Programs. Buffalo, NY: Prometheus Books, 1992.

Niall Coggans and
Susan McKellar

The Facts About Alcohol, Aggression, and Adolescence. New York: Cassell, 1995.

Eileen V. Coughlin, ed.

Successful Drug and Alcohol Prevention Programs. San Francisco: Jossey-Bass, 1994.

Norman K. Denzin

The Alcoholic Society: Addiction and Recovery of the Self. New Brunswick, NJ: Transaction Publishers, 1993.

Timothy Donohue

In the Open: Diary of a Homeless Alcoholic. Chicago: University of Chicago Press, 1996.

Jerry Dorsman

How to Quit Drinking Without AA: A Complete Self-Help Guide. Newark, DE: New Dawn, 1993.

Scott Dowling, ed.

The Psychology and Treatment of Addictive Behavior. Madison, CT: International Universities Press, 1995.

Emma Fossey

Growing Up with Alcohol. New York: Routledge, 1994.

Vince Fox

Addiction, Change, and Choice: The New View of Alcoholism. Tucson, AZ: See Sharp Press, 1995.

Jonathan Harris

This Drinking Nation. New York: Four Winds Press, 1994.

Dwight B. Heath, ed.

International Handbook on Alcohol and Culture. Westport, CT: Greenwood Press, 1995.

Harold D. Holder and
Griffith Edwards, eds.

Alcohol and Public Policy: Evidence and Issues. New York: Oxford University Press, 1995.

George S. Howard
and Peter E. Nathan, eds.

Alcohol Use and Misuse by Young Adults. Notre Dame, IN: University of Notre Dame Press, 1994.

Lloyd D. Johnston

National Survey Results on Drug Use from Monitoring the Future Study, 1975–1994. Rockville, MD: National Institute on Drug Abuse, 1995.

Jean Kinney and
Gwen Leaton

Loosening the Grip: A Handbook of Alcohol Information. Saint Louis: Mosby, 1995.

Audrey Kishline   *Moderate Drinking: The Moderation Management Guide for People Who Want to Control Their Drinking.* New York: Crown Trade Paperbacks, 1994.

Caroline Knapp   *Drinking: A Love Story.* New York: Dial Press, 1996.

Mike Males   *The Scapegoat Generation: America's War on Adolescents.* Monroe, ME: Common Courage Press, 1996.

Brian Maracle   *Crazywater: Native Voices on Addiction and Recovery.* New York: Penguin, 1994.

George McGovern   *Terry: My Daughter's Life-and-Death Struggle with Alcoholism.* New York: Villard, 1996.

Kenneth J. Meier   *The Politics of Sin: Drugs, Alcohol, and Public Policy.* Armonk, NY: M.E. Sharpe, 1994.

Judy Monroe   *Alcohol.* Hillside, NJ: Enslow Publishers, 1994.

Robert Nash Parker   *Alcohol and Homicide: A Deadly Combination of Two American Traditions.* Albany: State University of New York Press, 1995.

Stanton Peele   *Diseasing of America: Addiction Treatment Out of Control.* Lexington, MA: Lexington Books, 1989.

Stanton Peele and Archie Brodsky, with Mary Arnold   *The Truth About Addiction and Recovery: The Life Process Program for Outgrowing Destructive Habits.* New York: Simon & Schuster, 1992.

Knud-Erik Sabroe   *Alcohol in Society: Patterns and Attitudes.* Aarhus, Denmark: Aarhus University Press, 1994.

Marc A. Schuckit   *Educating Yourself About Alcohol and Drugs: A People's Primer.* New York: Plenum, 1995.

Jean Bonnie Stanley   *The Message: Living Happy—Joyous—and Free: Legacy of the Twelve Steps.* San Diego, CA: Heartfelt Books, 1995.

Jack Trimpey   *Rational Recovery: The New Cure for Substance Addiction.* New York: Simon & Schuster, 1996.

Jack Trimpey   *The Small Book: A Revolutionary Alternative for Overcoming Alcohol and Drug Dependence.* Rev. ed. New York: Dell, 1996.

George E. Vaillant   *The Natural History of Alcoholism Revisited.* Cambridge, MA: Harvard University Press, 1995.

Henry Wechsler et al.   *Secondary Effects of Binge Drinking on College Campuses.* Newton, MA: Higher Education Center for Alcohol and Other Drug Prevention, 1996.

Thomas S. Weinberg   *Gay Men, Drinking, and Alcoholism.* Carbondale: Southern Illinois University Press, 1994.

James Wiley   *Power Recovery: The Twelve Steps for a New Generation.* New York: Paulist Press, 1995.

Index